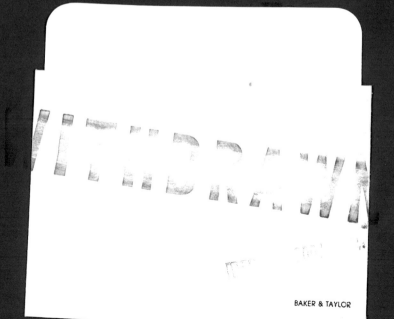

Florida A&M University, Tallahassee
Florida Atlantic University, Boca Raton
Florida Gulf Coast University, Ft. Myers
Florida International University, Miami
Florida State University, Tallahassee
University of Central Florida, Orlando
University of Florida, Gainesville
University of North Florida, Jacksonville
University of South Florida, Tampa
University of West Florida, Pensacola

A SEMINOLE LEGEND

The Life of Betty Mae Tiger Jumper

Betty Mae Tiger Jumper and Patsy West

University Press of Florida

Gainesville · Tallahassee · Tampa · Boca Raton

Pensacola · Orlando · Miami · Jacksonville · Ft. Myers

06   05   04   03   02   01   6   5   4   3   2   1

Library of Congress Cataloging-in-Publication Data
Jumper, Betty Mae, 1923–.
A Seminole legend: the life of Betty Mae Tiger Jumper /
Betty Mae Tiger Jumper and Patsy West.
p. cm.
Includes bibliographical references and index.
ISBN 0-8130-2285-1
1. Jumper, Betty Mae, 1923–. 2. Seminole Indians—Biography.
3. Seminole Indians—History. I. West, Patsy, 1947–. II. Title.
E99.S28 J86   2001
975.9004'973'0092—dc21   2001027352

The University Press of Florida is the scholarly publishing agency for the State
University System of Florida, comprising Florida A&M University, Florida Atlantic
University, Florida Gulf Coast University, Florida International University, Florida
State University, University of Central Florida, University of Florida, University
of North Florida, University of South Florida, and University of West Florida.

University Press of Florida
15 Northwest 15th Street
Gainesville, FL 32611–2079
http://www.upf.com

Contents

Photographs appear on pages 79–100.

First Preface

I wrote this book because people would be curious about this history, my story, in years to come. They would be wondering how things were. In this book they will learn how our family history evolved.

People thought my family was "bad medicine" because we were half-white. When I became useful to the tribe as an interpreter and later as a nurse, they realized how important my job was to show them the new ways. My family members were tribal pioneers in changing times.

I dedicate this book to my mother and family.

Betty Mae Jumper

Second Preface

In 1995 I presented a paper on Betty Mae Jumper at the annual meeting of the Florida Historical Society in Tallahassee. Following an enthusiastic reception, Seminole War historian John K. Mahon said adamantly that this paper should be published. When, months later, I received a call from an excited Betty and her insistent friend Tom Foche on their way home from the West, asking if would I collaborate with Betty on her "life story," I was thrilled to be afforded the opportunity.

Betty is very well known to Floridians as a storyteller. Academics generally zero in on the fact that she is the only woman who has served as chair, or "chief," of the Seminole Tribe of Florida (1967–71). They consider this accomplishment to surpass by far anything else she has ever done. In lengthy conversations with Betty, however, I learned that being chief of the Seminole Tribe of Florida was not on the top of Betty's list of her greatest personal accomplishments. Her benchmark of accomplishment was the driving spirit and determination that launched her on a course to obtain an education—the accomplishment of a fourteen-year-old child who had the nerve to beg to leave the safe haven of her grandmother and her chickee for a foreign world on a major self-imposed quest.

Betty Mae Jumper's handwritten manuscript, which she compiled over the period between 1953 and 1972, forms the basis of *A Seminole Legend: The Life of Betty Mae Tiger Jumper*. The sheets of lined paper, handwritten, on topical subjects, came to me with corresponding typed pages from a secretary. Corrections between the handwritten pages and the typescript had been meticulously initialed by Betty. Most of the manuscript was written during her period as chair of the tribe. This valuable material escaped the fire that ravaged Betty's home in the 1970s only because it was in her desk at tribal headquarters.

It is a compelling narrative, poignant, sometimes heartrending, but with the strength and determination that seem to characterize this family and are personified by author, storyteller, and activist Betty Mae Jumper.

In addition to Betty's manuscript, sources used in the preparation of this book include my interviews with Betty (in May 1991, September 1995, and twelve interviews during the period from March 1998 to October 1999), collections of newspaper clippings, and other historical documents. Much of the documentary material was preserved by important players in Seminole social welfare organizations. In a real sense these longtime advocates whom Betty knew and admired are aiding the Florida Seminoles once more. Their valuable resource material covers many aspects of Betty's life as well as the life of the Seminole people on the Hollywood Reservation.

The major sources are a newspaper clipping service from the Seminole Indian Association, W. Stanley Hanson (founder), secretary (1927–37), provided by the W. Stanley Hanson, Jr., family of Ft. Myers to the Seminole/Miccosukee Photographic Archive; the Ann Palmer Sheldon Pressbook, made while she was chairwoman of the Florida Federation of Women's Clubs' Indian Committee (1950s), in the collection of the Broward County Historical Commission; and the papers of the Ft. Lauderdale–based Friends of the Seminoles, Ivy

C. Stranahan (founder) (1930s to 1960s), and Jane Kirkpatrick donation, Ft. Lauderdale Historical Society, which were invaluable in reconstructing the reservation period in which Betty was involved.

I have contributed research material on Betty's newsworthy ancestors and set her narrative in the broader perspective of twentieth-century Florida Seminole history. Her story is both personal and profoundly valuable as a compelling discussion and insightful perspective of Seminole tribal history, which has been thus far unwritten for lack of a native voice, a voice that Betty Mae Jumper has now provided.

Patsy West

Introduction

A growing number of Native American women have realized the importance of their own experiences and are actively contributing to the compendium of information that constitutes Native American women's studies. While often culturally reticent about sharing their life experiences, they are beginning to see the impact that the story of their lives can have on others, most important on their own people, those children growing up and those yet to be born. The elders' lives were lived on the brink between the old ways and the new: the Indian religion and Christianity, the government's Indian schools which enforced assimilation, and the more nurturing and culturally enhanced educational environments of today.

Younger women writers see the value of discussing their own generations' struggles with life on the reservations, substance abuse, abject poverty, government bureaucracy. Some of them were participants in historic Native American events in the 1970s such as Wounded Knee or Alcatraz, which aided in calling attention to Native American rights issues. They want to share the harsh existence of life on reservations as they tried to raise children and follow traditions in a changing, poverty-stricken community where the main attraction was alcohol and death was commonplace. Still others were raised in nonreservation communities and discuss the remembering, maintaining, or even relearning of their Native American tribal heritage.

All Native American tribes are different, and the stories the women tell are widely diverse. Yet today they collectively form a corpus of Native American women's literature, and the information is of vital importance to all tribal histories.

[Among Native American Indian tribes, the Florida Seminoles are unique. Thus the saga of a Florida Seminole family as told by Betty Mae Jumper is a most valuable contribution. From her narrative, which spans over 150 years, little-known eras of Seminole history are illuminated which are of fundamental importance to an overall understanding of the people who call themselves the Florida Seminoles.

Topics discussed include culture, sociopolitical roles, miscegenation, war atrocities, the introduction and impact of Christianity, non-Indian support groups. They combine to give a rare insight into Seminole life as it was and the changes that it has had to confront. *A Seminole Legend: The Life of Betty Mae Tiger Jumper* will have a significant place in Native American literature. Betty will join the ranks of those women who have taken the responsibility for documenting their family histories and are responsible, in the process, for recording an important component of their collective tribal history.]

Authors' Note

[To differentiate between authors, Betty Mae Jumper's narrative is italicized, while Patsy West's text appears in Roman type.]

1

The Snake Clan
Returns to Florida

By 1740 the first Native Americans who would be known as the Seminole Indians had moved into the Spanish-held Florida peninsula from southern Alabama and Georgia, bringing with them their Creek heritage. Spain's hold on the Florida territory was weak, and as a result the Seminoles thrived in Florida on the frontier of international politics. By the early 1800s the Seminole chiefs' large herds of cattle and sedentary life had attracted runaway African slaves, who attached themselves to the chiefs as new masters and protectors. The southeastern Indians had enjoyed a long tradition of slaveholding. The Seminoles readily accepted the influx of Africans, who served them well by working in the fields and with the Seminole cattle herds.

However, the valuable commodities of cattle and slaves would put the Seminoles in danger. The First Seminole War (1817–18) was little more than a border conflict between the southern plantation owners and the Seminoles over the ownership of cattle and slaves. The plantation owners instigated raids on Seminole towns to steal cattle that

Set-up | history to give setting | understanding to Tiger's manuscript.

they claimed from the Seminole chiefs' ample herds and to retrieve runaway slaves who had taken refuge among the Seminoles.

Under General Andrew Jackson, major raids to the Mikasuki towns as far south as Alachua (Gainesville) were successful. Slaves and cattle were confiscated, while the large Seminole settlements were destroyed. The majority of the uprooted Seminoles fled south, some as far south as Tampa Bay and the Everglades.

As a result of Jackson's unauthorized raid into Spanish Florida, he received harsh criticism, but the result of his brashness was that Spain relinquished Florida to the United States. Florida became a territory in 1821. Jackson briefly held the position of Florida's military governor. He then was elected the nation's seventh president in 1829, serving two terms. In 1830 he instituted his Indian removal policy, which would affect all southeastern Indians residing east of the Mississippi. They would be forcibly removed to Indian Territory, located in present-day Oklahoma.

The Choctaws, Chickasaws, and even the more acculturated Cherokees of Georgia were rounded up and marched on the long, arduous Trail of Tears en route to the Indian Territory. Hunger, disease, and the rigors of the journey decimated many prior to their arrival on their reservations, while others succumbed in the new country to which they were not accustomed. The Florida Seminoles were the only tribe to offer armed resistance, and the Second Seminole War lasted seven years (1835–42).

At the outset of Betty Mae Jumper's narrative, the Second Seminole War was well under way. The Seminole population was weary, but a welcome period of peace prevailed on both sides, because the U.S. military thought that a treaty agreement had been made that would end the war.

Everyone was saying it was peace at last. The soldiers quit chasing the Seminoles and promised to leave them alone. The interpreter told the Indians, "The white man said it is ended. No more fighting." So the Indians began to settle down and make homes and plant things.

During the Second Seminole War, there was a short truce. It was created from the signing of the Macomb Treaty, a document made with a presumed overall leader of the Seminoles in 1837. General Thomas Jesup then waited on the capitulation of major Seminole chiefs following the treaty agreement. One group of Seminoles was in Tampa awaiting deportation to Indian Territory, and by April Jesup considered the war to be over. However, many bands of Seminoles never knew of the treaty as they had not been involved in its making. Soon it became obvious that the treaty agreement was invalid, and the war continued for another five years (Mahon 1967:200–204).

The Macomb Treaty encompassed the spring planting months of January to June. This time of presumed peace could have been when the Snake clan encamped on the river near today's Jupiter, Florida, and began to settle down to peacetime camping.

One day when most of the men were out hunting, soldiers suddenly came and surrounded a camp of Seminoles [i:laponi:, Mikasuki people], mostly old men, women, and children, along a river. That is why the river there was from that day on called "Lo-tsa-hatchee," meaning "River of Lies" in Creek, because our people thought that peace had been made. The soldiers gathered the Indians like criminals, making them all sit down in the open fields. Some were lucky enough to run away, and those who escaped ran to other camps to warn them. [The "River of Lies" is today the "River of Turtles" changed over the century from "Lo-tsa" to the "Loxahatchee."]

After the captives were rounded up, they were made to walk toward the west. The people were told, "The soldiers are going to put you in big boats and send you across the big, big water where you will never come back." After days of walking, they reached the big boat [probably at Egmont Key]. *They were made to get on the boat, and they sailed off. While they were out at sea, they knew that they weren't being taken straight across the water* [as the soldiers had told them] *because when they went far off, the boat turned again. It went about two days traveling toward the west, then it turned east again. The Seminoles knew how to read their direction by looking at the moon, stars, and sun, so they knew that they were coming back to land on the same side.* [The captives were puzzled by this, but the boat was a steamer, which had to keep coming to shore to take on wood for its boilers.]

Finally the boat landed [perhaps in North Florida or as far away as Louisiana]. *The captives were hauled off like cattle and made to march to a big cage which had been made for them to stay in until they were forced to walk again.*

My great-great-grandmother and her three daughters were among those captives on board. In the pen where they were kept, she grew more and more worried, because the soldiers had begun using the younger women. She was concerned for her daughters. Then, she and her oldest daughter were raped, and she became consumed with a plan to help her youngest daughters escape. She dug a hole under the fence and sat on it all day so the soldiers wouldn't see. That night, she pushed the two youngest daughters through the hole to make their escape.

She had told them to run straight to the deep creek nearby which ran east and west. "Get in the water and swim toward the east quietly." She told them to put leaves on their heads and drift by, passing the place where the lookout soldier was standing. "He won't know you are passing by, as he will be looking at us." She was right. Paleface was on the bank, but he didn't look at the creek and never saw them pass by because as soon as she saw the girls disappear in the darkness, she started singing real loud. The other Indians joined her, making all of the soldiers turn to look at them. By this time the girls started to swim toward the bank on the south side. They knew the singing was a sign to get out and run.

That first night they ran most of the way, and by morning they were miles away. They slowed down by daylight and stopped to rest. With sunup they rejoiced, as the sun came up on their left side, and they knew that they were going in the right direction.

Through the wilderness, the girls traveled night and day trying to get back to their father and brothers. At times they were so tired that they fell down and slept. Cuts and scratches on their bodies did not slow them down. They hoped that they wouldn't happen on wild animals, but at an early age they had been taught to avoid such dangers. They could climb tall trees and hide, or jump in a river, and they carried a hard wood stick to hit them with.

The little food that they found consisted of small land turtles and water turtles, which they roasted on a small fire made in a pit in the ground. They cooked in the middle of the day, so no one would see the smoke. After roasting the meat, they covered the fire and put dead leaves over the ground. Everything was buried so that nothing would give them away, should soldiers be about. As a result, they did not cook much, but lived on wild berries, fruits, and palm cabbage. The cabbage they pulled from the center of the plant, the heart, where it is soft and delicious. Sometimes they found a pond of fish where the water was low and they could catch enough to make a meal.

The girls were excellent swimmers, but often the rivers they had to cross were too wide or very swift. When they had to cross a large river, they hunted for logs that would float. They would hang on and paddle across.

The thing that troubled them the most was the memories of their mother and sister who were left behind. Nighttime, when they lay down to sleep, was the worst time. They couldn't help but think of the circumstances under which they had left them and wonder how they were. They cried as they thought of the suffering of their older sister, who had been raped so much that she could hardly walk. The girls envisioned their mother carrying her. They could only hope that they were dead. It hurt them to think that way, but they knew their mother and sister would then be at peace. They recalled their mother saying, "Just look ahead and don't look back or turn back. Keep running toward the sun until you see your brothers and father," The girls had never disobeyed their mother before in their lives, but this request was the hardest to obey, as they would never see her again.

Their abused sister had told them, "Go like Mother says and don't stop. See me. The soldiers will start on you two next, so leave when Mother says. These men have no pity on anyone, young or old. They are like wild beasts. They treat us like animals. They laugh and kick you around while raping you and make a big joke out of it in front of others. They drive us like cows on the trail. You have seen when older people get sick or too tired to walk. They fall. They get whipped and are made to get up. If they are too helpless to get up and walk, the soldiers shoot them. If babies cry too much from being hungry, the soldiers throw them in a creek or pond and drown them or hit them against a tree to kill them. Every Indian that lives through this sorrowful march, this nightmare, can never live the rest of their lives in peace. Leave! Run for your lives. You'll be free!"

On the fourth day they saw a chickee, but they were scared to go near it. They saw pigs roaming around the camp, but no people. In one chickee they saw belongings scattered around. They thought that the people must have left very fast. Maybe they were chased off. The girls knew that there must be food in the cooking chickee, and they found dried meat hanging over the fireplace. One sister commented that it was odd to see everything in its place like people were there, but there was no one. Finding the food, they built a little fire and roasted the dry meat to eat. They had been hungry for so long. They went to the chickees and took some of the clothes, which they needed badly. Then they went to a pond nearby to take a bath and put on the new clothes. But they were apprehensive because the pigs followed them around. They knew that the pigs would give away their presence if they needed to hide. To get rid of the pigs, they pulled down a bag of corn and left more corn where the pigs would find it. Then they took some bedding and ran into the woods. With a good meal and soft bed, they slept hard. The sun was up high before they awoke. They gathered food from the camp, put more corn down to distract the pigs, and ran on.

The sun was going down when they heard a noise like someone yelling in the distance. They were scared and climbed a big oak tree. The tree was so big that they lay against a branch and slept part of the night. The next morning they came down and started walking. They heard sounds again and walked more cautiously. Many birds were flying around, so they knew that they were near the water. They climbed a tree to see what was ahead of them and saw someone walking in an open field.

They got down from the tree and approached cautiously, hearing the sounds of people talking. Soon a camp materialized in the middle of the woods with a few women and men and children sitting around. The sisters peered through the bushes at them for a long time, trying to see if they recognized *anyone. Finally, they made their way to the camp. Some children spotted them and yelled, "Hey! Hey! Someone is coming!"*

A man came to talk to them and found out that they were Mikasuki girls. The men had seen their father and brothers on the south side of Lake Okeechobee a few days before. The girls were welcomed in the camp and were told to eat and rest before they set out to meet up with their family. They had been gone two months!

The next morning, two young men from the camp rounded up four horses to ride, gathered up supplies, and they started out early with the girls to travel around the lake. The boys said that there had not been soldiers in the area for months, so it was safe. They couldn't believe that the Snake girls had been able to make it back home after being taken so far away.

On the third day they met a hunter who was out looking for deer. He told them of a camp about half a day's ride east along a river. He thought that the girls' father and brothers were there, because people who had been hiding out in the Everglades had been coming in for days. They found their father and brothers! The girls cried and told their sad tale, and the camp mourned.

This is a true story told to me by my grandmother Mary Tustenuggee Tiger. Because of these brave sisters, the Snake clan did not disappear, but that's why there aren't very many people in our clan. After the wars ended, the Snake girls married. But since there were only two girls, the Snake clan remained small, as only the women carry their clan to their children. The Snake girls had children, but some of my grandmother's sisters did not marry.

Today there are about forty-five people in the Snake clan. There are mostly boys now, and they cannot carry on their clan to their children. But however small, the Snake clan still continues.

2

The Tustenuggees and the Bluefields Massacre

Wartime family oral histories, such as Betty's grandmother's account, provide rare examples for literature. This narrative is only the second for a Seminole–related escape in the Second Seminole War period that has been published (see deVane 1978:340–42). War stories provided tribal history and entertainment. They also served to keep Seminole children from integrating with non-Indians, as the nature of the sagas, passed down from generation to generation, reinforced a distrust of whites and kept alive the horror of wartime and wartime atrocities. As a result, the Seminoles emerged with extreme reticence toward outsiders and an overt wariness of being tricked and taken to Oklahoma, a fear that lasted far into the twentieth century (West 1998b:8–9, 60, 61).

Approximately one-third of the postwar Seminole population was Muscogee-speaking Creeks, who had come into Florida following their defeat by Andrew Jackson at the Battle of Horseshoe Bend in 1814. Betty's grandmother Mary Tustenuggee's family, however, were

Mikasuki speakers, or *i:laponi:*, who had settled in Florida earlier, around 1750. The cultures were similar, stemming from the Creek traditions of southern Alabama and Georgia. In fact, Creek was the formal or diplomatic language of the Mikasuki people (who call themselves *i:laposhni: cha thi* or *i:laponathli:*). The Creek, or Muscogee, language died out as a second language of the *i:laponathli:* only in the first half of the twentieth century. (Muscogee survives today as the language of approximately one-third of the members of the Seminole Tribe of Florida [Sturtevant 1971:112–13].)

By the Third Seminole War (1855–58) Betty's great-grandmother and her sister had married two Panther clan brothers. The Snake sisters had married well. Their husbands became important medicine men and political leaders. According to Smithsonian investigator Clay MacCauley, Kotsa Tustenuggee and his younger brother, Hospa-ta-ki, had been honored with the title *Tus-te-nug-ul-ki*, or "great warriors" of the tribe (Casey/Bowlegs 1850–53:13; MacCauley 1887: 469–531, 508–9).

Following the Third Seminole War the great-grandmother's Snake camp had returned to the settlement on Wild Island. Then, around 1868, the Wild Island Snake clan settlement moved to Fisheating Creek, seven or eight miles down the creek east of Palmdale (West 1995a).

Frederick Ober described the large Tustenuggee settlement thirty miles west of Indian River in which the Tustenuggees were encamped. The settlement contained thirty-two chickees and included a Green Corn Dance ground (Ober 1875:142, 171). The old camps were laid out this way, in a settlement pattern of groups of clans living in a defined settlement area. By the 1880s these areas were designated by locals and thus in the literature by a physical feature nearby, such as the Cow Creek settlement or the Catfish Lake settlement. Since the Snake clan was residing on Fisheating Creek, they became known as the Fisheating Creek settlement.

The Green Corn Dance grounds were integrated into the large settlements during this period. At the Corn Dance, all legal matters were discussed. During the 1874 Corn Dance, Tustenuggee was reinstated by the Seminole council to his hereditary position of "chief" of the Seminoles. That position had been held during and after the Second Seminole War by strong, nonhereditary leaders from the Panther clan. They had valiantly supported a strong resistance-to-removal movement during the Seminole wars in opposition to Micanopy, the weak hereditary chief whom they had "dethroned" during the Second Seminole War. But in 1874 Tustenuggee showed proof to the Seminole council that he was a descendant of Micanopy's royal line, and he was voted in. One witness stated, "That came near making a fight!" (Ober 1875:172; West 1992:365). Today, the Corn Dance is still an important activity for traditional Seminoles and is their major annual socioreligious celebration.

On another visit, Ober found the Tustenuggee family on a "grand hunt." He enthusiastically described their temporary lodging:

An Indian camp, in this village, moved into the forest, minus the houses. Hogs, dogs, hens, cooking-utensils, and every thing movable, is taken with them on a grand hunt. This party was destined for the prairies of the St. Johns [River], intending to be gone a month and procure hundreds of deer skins. They marched by easy stages, and hunted as they went. They were to stop here a few days to kill a couple of bears in the cypress-swamps near, then would move on.

Tied to a tree near my head is a half-grown bear. . . . Two small pigs are tied by the middle to another tree. . . . A litter of puppies, with their eyes yet unopened, snarl and whine beneath the shade of a palmetto. Upon poles, stretched from tree to tree, are piles of deer skins, and large bear-hides curiously stretched with sticks and thongs. From the trees hang pots and kettles, spoons, dippers, blankets, bladders, bottles, fawn-skins of honey, deer brains wrapped in moss, leggings, saddles, saddlebags, bear-meat in huge flakes, axes, knives, and thongs, and as miscellaneous and varied a wardrobe of feminine garments as ever adorned an Indian camp. (Ober 1875:172)

But in the fall of 1878, major changes were in store for the Tustenuggee women's Fisheating Creek settlement. The first herd of cattle was driven into the area by cattleman Jacob Summerlin. The area south from Okeechobee to Punta Rassa would come to be called Ninety Mile Prairie and would be prized by cattle interests for its prime pasturage (West 1995c:30).

The Snake clan settlement, consisting of around thirty persons, as well as other Seminole settlements in the region, thrived alongside the cattle interests at Fisheating Creek, raising herds of cattle and droves of hogs. But in the 1880s Captain John Whidden of Arcadia bought the C-5 stock of cattle from Summerlin. The cattle industry, the state's earliest and most important business, was growing. In those days of open range, space and ownership of livestock were considerations of life-threatening proportions. This was something that the Seminoles understood, as cattle and range had been important catalysts in their initial conflict with the United States, the First Seminole War (1817–18), and, as the power of the state's cattle barons grew, the Third Seminole (1855–58), which was fresh in their memory.

Captain Whidden thought that the area was getting too crowded and made an offer to the area Seminole families: he would buy out their stock if they would relocate. What the Seminoles' true feelings were on this issue is not known; they apparently accepted the offer. However, this business transaction served to displace a sizable percentage of the Seminoles and depopulate the historic *i:laponki:*, or Mikasuki, settlement on Fisheating Creek (West 1995c:30).

Interestingly enough, relations between the cattlemen and the Seminoles were generally amicable even though the Third Seminole War had placed them on opposite sides. Obviously the population of Seminoles had been reduced to the point that they posed no threat, yet for the most part the cattlemen and the Seminoles saw eye to eye, with mutual respect for the cow as the probable common denominator.

The sale completed, the Snake camp moved north to construct a new settlement at Addison, later called Bluefields, northeast of Lake Okeechobee. It was there that a major postwar tragedy occurred.

Historically, southeastern Indians maintained Indian slaves and made raids for the express purpose of obtaining them. Before and during the Seminole wars, the Seminole ruling families were major slaveholders, with (African or African-American) slaves, cattle, and horses recorded as their most valuable assets.

Following the Third Seminole War, only three slaves—all of them African-American women—remained with the Florida Seminoles. It has been documented that these individuals were first-generation African-Americans purchased as children by their Seminole masters. By the 1880s they were middle-aged. Some or all of their offspring (whether African-American or part-Seminole) continued to live in the Seminole settlements. Investigator Clay MacCauley noted "seven persons of mixed blood" living with the Seminoles in 1880 (1887:526; West 1995b).

In all accounts, the African-American slave women continued serving their Seminole masters and mistresses. They reared their own offspring within the parameters of Seminole culture. However, the Seminoles themselves were prejudiced against the African-American bloodline, and they commonly related to whites that the half-breeds were "Ho-la wa-gus" (no good).

Miscegenation with whites was not tolerated at all. A Seminole woman who gave birth to a half-white child was immediately killed by hanging. This was the worst possible death for a Seminole, for hanging did not allow the soul to leave the body through the mouth and thus get to heaven. The newborn child was also killed; a clanswoman would put sand or mud in its mouth or throw the infant into a body of water. The stigma against children born of illicit unions persisted well into the first decades of the twentieth century (Moore-Willson 1910:114; deVane 1955).

The few Seminole-black offspring of Seminole paternity were begrudgingly tolerated, but technically, and of great importance in their future relations within Seminole culture, the black mothers had no clan. However, the last three Seminole slaves were "given" the clan of their Seminole mistresses, which they in turn passed on to their offspring and thus to tribal descendants living today (Seminole Agency, Florida 1977).

The Snake clan owned the slave known as Nagey Nancy. Her children, Jim Jumper (Nigger Jim) and Nancy, of Seminole paternity, were given the designation of Little Black Snake. Nagey Nancy's daughter, Nancy, had two children by Seminole fathers: Billy Bowlegs III, whose father was the *i:laponi:* (Mikasuki-speaking Seminole) Billy Fewell (Wind clan), and his half-sister Lucy Bowlegs (later Pierce), whose father was Charlie Peacock (Deer). The Snake clan settlement was the only home these part-African-American, part-Seminole children and grandchildren would ever know (West 1995a).

Mary Tiger, Betty Mae Tiger's grandmother, was present and played a role in this saga. She passed down to her granddaughter Betty the following oral history account of the massacre that occurred on February 15, 1889.

Grandmother said that she had been pounding cornmeal near the camp when she heard the shots. Other women were preparing deer hides, as it was hunting season and the men were once again away on a hunt. Nancy [Billy Bowlegs's mother] ran over to Grandmother and said, "He's a crazy man, we should grab him [Jim Jumper]!" This was the women's job if a man caused a disturbance in their settlement. Grandmother and Nancy wrestled him down, but they didn't have a rope to tie him up. Everyone else was either dead or had run away with their children into the bushes. They tried to talk with Jim, to calm him down and reason with him, but he babbled things they couldn't understand. They finally realized that they couldn't hold him much longer, and Nancy said to Grandmother, "He's my brother. He can shoot me if he wants. You run." So while Nancy struggled with her half-brother, Grandmother grabbed up her two sons and ran as fast as she could to a hiding place.

More shots rang out. Grandmother could only imagine what they meant. Then it was quiet. She heard someone call out,

"He's dead! He's dead! You can come out!" But she clutched her sons closer and kept hiding. She waited a long time, until someone came near and told her it was all over and the murderer was dead. (Jumper 1995; West 1995b)

Billy Bowlegs III was not present at the Bluefields massacre, but in later years he related his personal tragedy to a friend who recorded it. Among those killed were his mother, Nancy, who had attacked Jumper with a knife; Old Tiger, also known as Woxo Micco or Cypress Tom Tiger, said to be the supreme leader of the Seminoles, who was visiting the Snake settlement with his Wind clan wife, a sister of Little Billie; Young Tiger, a medicine man and older brother of Captain Tom Tiger; Young Tiger's wife, Martha Tiger; and Jimmy Tiger. A half-brother of Bowlegs was thought to be dead, but he was revived (Stout 1965).

The tragedy at Bluefields was also witnessed by nine-year-old Will Addison, the elder son of settler John Addison. The family lived near Cypress Creek, only a mile and a half from the Snake settlement. On the day of the massacre Mrs. Addison had gone with Will to the camp of two traders, named Cuneo and Hendrix, which was within sight of the Seminole settlement. She was looking for a shawl blanket for her new baby, Tom.

Will later recalled that he and his mother were looking over the traders' wares at their wagon when Jim Jumper passed by on his way to the Seminole camp. Mrs. Addison noticed that he had a bad wound on the calf of his leg. She thought that he might have been gored by the tusks of a wild hog in a hunting accident. She questioned Jim about his leg, but he answered sullenly that he "didn't know."

Will recalled: "In a few minutes we heard shooting, several shots, one after another. I looked across the prairie from behind a ledge of cabbage palms and saw Jim Jumper shoot the chief's squaw [Lucy]. He chased her around an ox cart. She was so big with child that she could hardly run. He headed her off and raised his rifle and fired, point blank. She fell down and died. We heard the squaws screaming warnings to their children. The children all scattered, going to cover like baby quail when a hawk swoops down." Jim Jumper killed his own half-sister [Billy Bowlegs's mother, Nancy], Lake Willson, Chief Woxo Micco, Big Tommie, and "an old Indian named Tiger" (Smiley 1964).

As is often the case with eyewitness accounts, young Addison's and Mary Tiger's reports differ, and Billie Bowlegs's assessment provides yet another perspective. Nevertheless, they serve to chronicle this tragic event, which further depleted the Snake clan and drastically reduced the total postwar Seminole population. The massacre at Bluefields was the most violent mass murder of Seminoles in the tribe's postwar history.

There were also a number of thought-provoking speculations as to why the massacre occurred. All of the accounts mention that Jim Jumper had asked to marry the daughter of Big Tommie but had been refused because he was black. Adding insult to injury was a remark reputedly made by Big Tommie's mother. She had recently died and had been interred standing in the crevice of a huge cypress tree. Prior to her death she reportedly had said that she wanted her slave Jim Jumper killed and "put with her" to serve her in the afterworld. At this time, favorite horses were still sometimes killed at the deceased's grave site, so Addison speculated that Jim Jumper might have thought that Grandmother Tommie's request would actually be carried out and he went crazy (Smiley 1964).

The bereaved Billy Bowlegs was told that Jumper had shot his mother while they quarreled, and when others intervened, Jumper shot them as well. But it seems that the catalyst for the rampage was the opposition to Jumper's proposal of an interracial marriage, a fact which was corroborated by cattleman Jacob Summerlin and supported by Addison's eyewitness account as well as this statement by Bowlegs: "When Jumper was told to find himself a Negro wife, he said no, he had been reared a Seminole and wanted a Seminole wife. Refused again, he got drunk," which resulted in the massacre (Stout 1965).

It is also possible that Jumper experienced a medical complication that contributed to his killing spree. Perhaps the bad wound that Mrs. Addison had noticed had become so badly infected that it caused fever and dementia—hence Jumper's incoherence noted in Mary Tiger's account. Decades later, noted Seminole medicine man Josie Billie stressed in a conversation with his friend W. Stanley Hanson that Jumper was "crazy," not "drunk" (Hanson 1943).

When Jumper's rampage was almost over, he shot at a little boy but missed. The child located Billy Martin tending a cane field nearby. As Martin approached the settlement, he saw Jumper "sitting on a log eating *sofkee*," and he shot the murderer with his .38 caliber, 1873 model Winchester" (Smiley 1964).

John Addison loaned the settlement a yoke of oxen and a wagon to use in disposing of the body (because the Seminoles did not want to spiritually "contaminate" their own possessions). "They put a rope around the corpse's neck and dragged it to a small cypress pond and threw it in for the gators to feed on" (Stout 1965). The Snake clan immediately packed up and moved their camp a short distance away and set up a temporary camp. Then Charlie Osceola (Panther), a medicine man, went to the massacre site, where he prepared medicine that would cleanse it and thus preserve the health of the survivors.

Addison recalled that every dog and chicken that tasted the blood of the victims was killed. A burial site for the persons slain was made nearby. Most important, because the area was tainted from the effects of violent death, the Snake clan settlement moved far away from the area along State Road 70 between Okeechobee and Ft. Pierce. This area came to be known as "Nigger Jim Scrub"(Smiley 1964).

3

Captain Tom Tiger

Mary Tiger—Betty Mae Tiger's grandmother who escaped the tragic massacre at the Bluefields settlement—was born in 1860, according to Seminole Agency records (1977:116). As a girl, Mary came to be known to townspeople as both Mary Tustenuggee (her father's surname) and Mary Gopher (the surname of her brother Jim Gopher).

At the time of her birth, the Third Seminole War had just ended, but the War Between the States had just begun. Although Florida saw little fighting during the war, the conflict had a great impact on the peninsula. The Union's naval blockade of Florida isolated the peninsula from a brisk trade with the Bahamas and Cuba so that no guns and ammunition would be smuggled in to support the Confederate cause, a situation that impoverished both settlers and Seminoles. Florida's major contribution to the war was its supply of cattle from the interior prairies, which were rounded up and driven north to feed the Confederate troops.

In about 1882 Mary Tustenuggee married a member of the Wild-cat clan named Cacha Launee, or Yellow Wildcat. More formally, he was called Micco Tustenuggee, but the townspeople called him "Captain" Tom Tiger (Moore-Wilson 1910:148).

Seminole society was matrilocal. Therefore Tom Tiger would have moved from the Wildcat/Panther settlement, where he was reared and where his mother and clan members resided, to live at his wife's mother's Snake clan settlement. There, all of the other Snake clan women, their husbands, their children, and unmarried brothers lived. The only outsiders were the women's husbands, who belonged to other clans. Marrying a member of their own clan was considered incest—a crime punishable by death.

Tom Tiger was described in the literature as an imposing figure and a Muscogee-speaking Seminole. A gregarious man, he was well known in the communities on the perimeters of the Seminole settlements and hunting areas. Most of his contemporaries, however, remained more aloof; they had little personal interaction with the white community north of Lake Okeechobee.

A few years after the Tigers were married, Mollie, Mary Tiger's younger sister, married Tom as well. It was a common practice for sisters to take the same husband. Indeed, some Seminole families were polygynous well into the twentieth century, a fact which was little known or discussed. Mary Tiger's first child was born in 1883 and Mollie's in 1886 (Seminole Agency, Florida 1977:116).

During his term of office (1881–85), President Chester A. Arthur visited Florida and fished on Lake Tohopekaliga on the Kissimmee River. He met with an official of the Okeechobee Improvement Company and viewed the results of the Everglades drainage project that the company had begun in the area. At Fort Gardner a landing was prepared so that the chief executive could disembark and meet with a family of Seminoles. It was Captain Tom Tiger and his two wives. President Arthur gave Tiger's baby 25 cents and gave Tom a cigar and a jackknife. As the president got ready to leave, he shook hands with Tom, who said, formally, "Come again. Glad to see Great Father" (*New York Times*, 1883).

In 1883 Tom Tiger was hired to lead a group of Seminoles to meet the first train arriving in Kissimmee on Plant's railroad. The *Lake City Reporter* wrote that "by prearrangement with Mr. Plant and to the amusement of his guests, Capt. Tom Tiger gave the war whoop" (de-Vane 1978:396). One result of Tiger's popularity was the appropriation of his photo for use on early postcards sold by Cochrane's Book Store in Palatka.

At first, relations between the postwar settlers and the Seminoles were good. But as more people arrived in Florida, relations sometimes became strained. Newcomers were apprehensive about the Indians. With no accurate census data available and with their imaginations at work, newspapermen in sleepy little towns quoted inflated numbers of "warriors who could rise up against them." This situation appears to have existed in all the towns along the Atlantic coast that had Seminole populations nearby in the Everglades interior.

Around Indian River, the settlers would have been very apprehensive had they known about the unsolved murder of the Shives family in 1872. This family had been brutally killed by the Seminoles in retaliation for a hunting incident in which a white hunter maliciously took the life of a Seminole hunter. The Shives were targeted only because they lived in the isolated house where the white hunter had previously resided (West 1995b).

By 1886 a number of settlers with unsavory backgrounds had put down roots in the locale east of Okeechobee. That year rustlers ran off cattle and hogs from the Cow Creek Seminole settlements east of the lake where the Tigers lived. Settlers from Ft. Pierce fled across the inland waterway to the House of Refuge out on the beach, as the Cow Creeks, deprived of their livestock, demanded $200 in damages or "would killum all, in two suns" (deVane 1978:333–34; Kersey 1974:49–58). Tom Tiger's role in this incident is not known, but certainly Tom, Mary, and Mollie Tiger were affected by it, for they knew the settlers and tradesmen.

Special Indian agent A. M. Wilson visited Tom Tiger and other Cow Creek Indians in November 1887 to help implement the government's program "to enable the Seminole Indians in Florida to obtain homesteads upon public lands and to settle themselves thereon," which had been outlined in the Indian Appropriation Act of July 4, 1884 (Senate Executive Document 139:1). Wilson had visited Tiger earlier in 1887 and commented in his report that he was "a very prominent and influential Indian, who upon our first visit had expressed a desire for a homestead and had also pledged us his influence in the matter." On Wilson's second trip, Tom was not at home, but one of his wives led Wilson to Tom's temporary camp, where he and his other wife were rounding up hogs. He agreed to act as a Wilson's guide in locating Seminole settlements to the south, but he did not follow through. Perhaps he sensed that the other Indians might not take kindly to his part in promoting the "Washington talk" (Senate Executive Document 139:8).

From 1898 to his untimely death in 1907, Tom Tiger held a unique role in the annals of Seminole history. As historian Bill McGown put it: "Without setting out to do so, Tom Tiger focused the nation's attention on the plight of Florida's Seminole Indians. . . . In life, he was the catalyst for the first non-Indian group dedicated to helping the tribe. In death, he set off the nearest thing Florida has had to a 20th century uprising" (McGown 1998:89).

In 1898 Tom Tiger was involved in an official complaint. In an unprecedented case, he accused a white man, Harmon Hull, of stealing his horse from the Snake settlement near Ft. Drum in December 1897. According to Tom, Hull had written on a cartridge box that he would return the horse in two months. When the two months were up, Tom's horse had not yet been returned and Hull's IOU had been obliterated by the elements. Tom confronted Hull, who flatly denied ever taking the horse. In June 1898 Tom told his friends James and Minnie Moore-Willson about his predicament. Minnie's book, *The Seminoles of Florida* (1896), provided a romanticized view of the tribe, but it did serve to alert the public to the tribe's desperate situation if land was not set aside for its use. In the person of Tom Tiger, Minnie had an example of a fine, upstanding Seminole who had been ill used. She threw her efforts into his case, using it to further the work of an organization that she and her husband had founded to protect Seminole rights and to obtain land for their permanent use. The Friends of the Florida Seminoles organization undertook litigation against Hull on Tiger's behalf (Kersey 1975:306–18).

"On the basis of a complaint filed by James Willson and attorney R. H. Seymore, Hull was charged with obtaining goods under false pretenses. Hull came to trial April 28, 1899, in Titusville.

"Though technically no Indians were parties to the case, Tiger and Bill Ham (Deer Clan) [Tiger's son-in-law] . . . did testify under oath, setting a precedent in Florida courts" (McGown 1998:91). Minnie Moore-Willson wrote that "Capt. Tom Tiger was the first Florida Indian that ever stood up in a white man's court, making, as the spectators remarked, the most imposing picture they had ever witnessed. The tall, magnificent-looking savage, with uplifted hand, took the oath on the Holy Book, with a perfect understanding of its meaning. . . . The Indian never swerved under the strongest cross-examination, but told the story simply and direct" (Moore-Willson 1910:148–49). (Taking into consideration that this event occurred more than 100 years ago, it is still interesting that Minnie, a vocal advocate for Seminole welfare, should refer to her friend Tiger as a "magnificent-looking savage.")

The white community rallied around Tom Tiger in unprecedented support, but with the main evidence obliterated and because neither Tiger nor Billy Ham could read, Judge M. S. Jones announced, "There was no case against Hull and instructed the jury to bring in a verdict of acquittal" (McGown 1998:91).

By this point, according to another account, Tom Tiger "had learned enough English to be employed in Indiantown, where for a time he was in charge of a store owned by Henry Brooker, the 'best known' of the hunters around Lake Okeechobee," according to historian Lawrence Will (Will 1964:90; Buswell 1972:329). If that statement is true, Tom may have been the first Seminole to hold such a job. No Seminole shopkeepers are noted in Harry A. Kersey, Jr.'s definitive publication on Seminole trade, *Pelts, Plumes, and Hides* (1975).

In 1906 Tom Tiger started hewing a canoe at the southern end of Brevard County. Apparently, the Tiger family's old cypress dugout canoe could no longer be repaired, and he needed a new, sturdy craft to navigate the lakes and rivers for hunting, trading, and visiting with his large family.

Canoemaking was an arduous but necessary task for every adult Seminole male. The first step was to select a large pond cypress, cut it down, and let it lie on the ground for several months to season. Then the time-consuming hewing process would begin; the Seminoles used an ax and adze, aided by charring with hot coals.

It would appear that Tom put in over two months' work. Another two to three weeks might have been enough for him to finish the canoe. One day, when a lightning storm was brewing, Tom was, perhaps, completing just one more task before the rain came, or maybe he had quit work and was picking up his tools. Whatever the case, he was struck by a bolt of lightning and died.

Tom's relatives did not move the body. While his wives mourned with their children at their settlement, Tiger's Wildcat/Panther clansmen cut the unfinished canoe in half lengthwise. Then they placed his body in one half of the canoe, and his clanswomen prepared him for his long journey to heaven, putting his pipe at his side. The other half of the canoe was turned over his body, and his personal belongings, including his adze, lantern, and gun, were placed on top. One of his male relatives fired a rifle in the air to the four directions in order to speed Captain Tom Tiger's soul to heaven; then the shooter tied the gun to a tree, and the group left. No one would ever use Tom Tiger's belongings again, as they belonged to him and should go with him over the bridge to heaven.

A captioned photograph in the National Anthropological Archives dated June 29, 1906, depicts "the deserted village of Tom Tiger's followers" (National Anthropological Archives, Smithsonian Institution 1906). Tom's family had moved away.

Tom Tiger was destined to be remembered for one more thing. In February 1907 a man by the name of John T. Flournoy came to the area looking for Seminole artifacts. He claimed affiliation with the Smithsonian Institution (*Ft. Myers Press* 1907b). Flournoy stayed with the family of Peter Raulerson, a Saint Lucie County commissioner who lived in the small town of Tantie. A trader by the name of Barber took Flournoy to show him Tom Tiger's isolated grave site. In the name of "science" Flournoy gathered up the bones of Captain Tom Tiger. The *St. Lucie County Tribune* (1907b) related the grizzly facts: "The grave was easily recognized from the pipe and other articles that were buried with him, and Mr. Flournoy proceeded to fill his hunting coat with the bones of the departed chief, taking the entire skeleton except the hands and feet which were too badly decayed to recover. He also took the noted pipe which the chief had smoked for many years. Mr. Flournoy told his companions that he intended to place the skeleton of Tom Tiger in the Smithsonian Institute." Flournoy and a box containing Tiger's bones left Ft. Pierce by train for the North.

On February 23, 1907, Billy Smith, the leading Cow Creek medicine man, came to Commissioner Raulerson. Smith reportedly told him, "Big Yankee—stole bones of Tom Tiger, Indian's big chief and best friend. Indians all fight. Kill white man ojus [plenty], bones no taken back by big Yankee by next moon" (*Ft. Myers Press* 1907a). Raulerson attempted to appease Smith with money, but the latter would not settle and reiterated his stand. Raulerson then reported the situation to the commission in Ft. Pierce. The commissioners sent the St. Lucie County sheriff, Dan L. Carlton, to the Seminole settlement to arrange "terms of peace." The Department of the Interior, the governor of Florida, and the federal commissioner in Miami were also contacted. On March 23, 1907, the *Ft. Myers Press* reported, "State's Attorney John C. Jones has filed information in the Circuit Court against one F. I. [*sic*] Flournoy, charging him with disturbing the grave of another and having in his possession a dead body."

The white settlers in the area experienced some anxious weeks. As soon as Billy Smith's threat became known, the *St. Lucie County Tribune* (1907b) noted that "the Indian temper is not a known quality, and should they all harbor the same feelings as expressed by their chief, our outlying sections may be in danger of annihilation at the hands of the outraged Indians." In his research, historian Harry A. Kersey, Jr., found that the youngest Raulerson children went to stay with relatives out of the immediate area, while residents of White City were issued extra ammunition and made plans to erect barricades at the entrance bridge into town (1974:54). Meanwhile, a Ft. Pierce shopkeeper capitalized on the situation by creating the following advertisement: "Kill White Man Ojus!"—So threatens Billie Smith, the Big Chief of the Seminoles, unless their demands are complied with —To Arms! To Arms!—We have them; also ammunition—The Fee & Stewart Co., Hardware and Undertaking—Ft. Pierce, Florida" (*St. Lucie County Tribune* 1907a).

Sheriff Carlton's meeting with Billy Smith had gone well. Smith had asked the sheriff how many moons it would take to get Tom Tiger's bones back. The sheriff had assured him that they would indeed be returned but convinced them that "this cannot be done by one moon." He promised to have them back in "three moons" (*St. Lucie County Tribune* 1907c; *Ft. Myers News Press* 1907a). The Fee & Steward Co. drew up another advertisement geared to scare the community into purchasing weapons and ammunition, just in case Sheriff Carlton's deal went sour (*St. Lucie County Tribune* 1907d).

Meanwhile, James Willson contacted the Smithsonian Institution on behalf of the Friends of the Seminoles organization. The Smithsonian's reply, published in the *Tribune* and in the second revised edition of Minnie Moore-Willson's book, noted that Flournoy had misled the Smithsonian Institution. Assistant Secretary Rathbun related in response to James Willson, "[Flournoy] wrote to the National Museum and offered to present certain Indian relics which he had obtained in Florida, including a skeleton of an Okeechobee (not Seminole) chief. Assuming that these objects were properly acquired by him, he was notified that they would be accepted [but Flournoy never sent them]" (*St. Lucie County Tribune* 1907d; Moore-Willson 1910:153–54).

Assistant Secretary Rathbun continued, saying that "although I find that the name of the chief was mentioned in Mr. [Flournoy]'s letter the fact that he spoke of him as belonging to the extinct Okeechobee tribe misled the Museum authorities who did not associate him with the Seminole Captain Tom Tiger, about whom so much has lately been printed in the papers until the receipt of your letter to-day.

"I cannot express too strongly my abhorrence of the act of Mr. [Flournoy], whose desecration of this grave I consider outrageous and sacrilegious. The man had no connection with this museum or any branch of the Smithsonian Institute, as he seems to have claimed several weeks before he sent in his letter."

From Flournoy's letterhead, Assistant Secretary Rathbun identified him as the general manager of an amusement park in Johnstown, Pennsylvania. He suggested, "It is not impossible that the relics were taken there" and offered the Smithsonian's cooperation "in securing the return of the remains" (*St. Lucie County Tribune* 1907d; Moore-Willson 1910:153–54).

To calm the citizens, some of whom had left the area or were considering such a move, Sheriff Carlton assured them, "There is as much danger of an Indian uprising as there is of a Hottentot invasion of England" (*St. Lucie County Tribune* 1907e).

Flournoy did return to Florida in three months with the bones. He arrived in June, apparently under the supervision of James Moore-Willson. The bones of Tom Tiger were again laid to rest, to the satisfaction of all parties.

However, due to a typographical error in the initial filing of the prosecution, Flournoy's initials were incorrect. The prosecution refiled. Because this unprecedented incident had by then been rectified, Flournoy was not prosecuted, and the matter is presumed to have been dropped (Kersey 1974:56). But the saga of Captain Tom Tiger remains unique in the annals of Florida history.

4

The Indian Missionaries' First Trip to Florida

Soon after Tom Tiger's death, his family was visited by a group of Indian missionaries from Oklahoma. Mary Tiger passed on to her granddaughter, Betty Mae Jumper, the story of the missionaries' journey to Florida, which Betty relates here.

In 1907 a train stopped at the quiet little town called Stuart, Florida. Seven people got off the train. A man, his wife, two kids, his friend, his wife, and another lady. These people were Christian Indians from Oklahoma whose great-grandmothers had left Florida on the Trail of Tears. They had volunteered to journey back to In-Con-Uck'seh, *which in the Creek language means "the edge of the land" that was Florida, to tell the good news that they had learned about this man who gave his life so that we may live forever.*

In 1845 the Southern Baptist Convention organized in the East, and by 1846 missionaries began to be sent to work among the Indian

tribes in the Southwest. In Oklahoma the tribes began to be Chris-
tianized largely through the efforts of the Home Mission Board of the
Southern Baptist Convention (Southern Baptist Convention n.d.:6;
Belvin n d.[1955]:13). But it was not until 1907 that the first Indian
missionaries, Creek speakers from Holdenville, Oklahoma, came east
to Florida in order to bring their "Jesus Road" teachings to their
brethren, the Florida Seminoles (West 1999).

*These Indians of Oklahoma knew that there were folks left behind in Flor-
ida. They knew that someone must return to tell them about the love of God
and who Jesus is. After many talks and prayers, these people were willing
to come back to the people of Florida. They knew that it would be hard to go
to the Indians of Florida, who have no use for people of the outside world.
They trust no one. But one preacher named Goat told the people: "I'll go. As
I pray, I know that Jesus wants me to go. Someone must go, and it's me. I'll
go with my family and take anyone else who wants to go."*

*After a few months of talk and prayers, the preacher, his wife, and their
two children, another couple, and a single woman were ready. Late one
evening, a train stopped at the siding of a little Oklahoma town, and these
people got on it. They had money that had been collected for them which
they expected would last five months. Their friends promised to send more
if it was needed. Slowly the train started puffing away toward the south.
When they would get to their destination, they didn't know. What kind of
greeting would they receive? They were apprehensive because they had heard
many tales of how Florida Indians were.*

*But before they left, an old man had come up to them and told them,
"My grandmother was left behind. Her name was so and so. Tell them of
your clan. Tell them that you know her relative. Tell them you know of her,
that I am her kin, and that you want to talk to her kin. Her family must
be left there. It was around the Big Lake [Okeechobee, "Big Water" in
Mikasuki] where they were left behind. They would be speaking in the Creek
language, so if you reach the lake, greet them in Indian. Do not talk the
white people's language. This would turn them off, and they wouldn't talk to*

you. But I know there must be some Indians who will accept you when they hear you talk in Indian."

After many days and nights of riding in the train, they reached Florida, where they saw many palmetto and orange trees. They got off at Stuart on a hot day at noon. At the town there were a few settlers, mostly farmers and trappers. After their belongings were gathered up, they went about a mile away and made camp under the trees. They rested for the afternoon and night because they were very tired from the long train ride.

It was summer, and they had heard it got pretty hot in Florida, but they were used to it, because Oklahoma gets real hot too. But they didn't know how they were going to take the mosquito bites.

After resting all night, they looked over their list. They had been advised to get two oxen to pull a wagon, one big wagon, one horse to ride places that would be too far to walk, food, cooking utensils, and a big tent to camp in. After getting all of their supplies from a store, they were ready to go. The people in town told them that they had better get enough food to last at least two months because "where you're heading, there is no store. The city of Okeechobee is thirty miles from where you will be. A boat comes once a month to a little store on the river where you are going to be. If you are not there when it comes in (people know when the boat is coming and wait for it to land), all of the supplies are gone on the first day." A lady said, "The people are not friendly where you are going. They keep to themselves pretty close."

The next morning they started off toward the west, toward the Big Lake. People in town said that it was a good two days' travel. Traveling was real slow with the wagon. [They were on the old Indiantown road. The former Military Trail, this curved and winding road, which traversed highlands and swamps, had been used during the Seminole wars to supply troops in the Okeechobee area (*Stuart News*, May 10. 1956).]

The first day, they traveled all day going west. They saw small animals and lots of ponds and streams where they saw turtles and fish. When evening began to fall and the sun was going down, they started looking for a place to camp and rest for the night. The family came to a place that looked good. After they started a fire, the women cooked the evening meal. Everyone was hungry and enjoyed it. After dinner they built a bigger fire, and everyone sat by it and listened to all kinds of noises from the night birds. Some seemed to be singing, but others just yelled! Then came the noise of an old owl. Then the birds began to sound like they were laughing; one started, and another in the distance answered back. The children wanted to know if they were laughing at them. "No," said their father, "They must be talking to each other in this manner because they are all answering each other in a funny, laughing tune." [Later accounts of pioneer settlers being bothered by panthers and wildcats on this very road can be read in the *Stuart News* (1956).]

The next day, they all got up early and started off after breakfast. As they were traveling, they watched the early morning animals eating or playing in the trees. They saw little squirrels climbing trees, while at a distance they saw a deer with a doe eating grass. Lots of birds were flying around, and a coon was sitting near a pond hunting food to eat. Rabbits sat nearby watching as they rode by. The missionaries guessed that many of the animals had never seen people before.

After hours of traveling, the sun passed the middle, so they decided to stop under a large tree near a lake and rest for a while before continuing their journey. When the food was ready, they gathered around and started eating.

Suddenly the little boy yelled, "Look! Someone is coming!" They all looked up. There was a man with a bundle on his back and a gun on his arm coming toward them. The preacher got up. He remembered what he had been told to do. He put out his hand and said, "Helth'ghe" (Hello) to him. Surprised, the man answered back and shook his hand. The newcomer was friendly and spoke in the Creek language. The missionaries invited him to eat, which he did.

They found out that he was a hunter who spent days at a time in the Glades hunting coon and gator hides to sell at the store for material for clothing, coffee, sugar, and flour, and deer meat to eat. (That hunter was one of my uncles!) They learned a great deal from the hunter. He told them that he lived in a little town called Indiantown. He said about fifty families of white and a few colored lived there with about twenty Indian families. The white settlers were farmers, cattlemen, fruit pickers, and workers in the cane fields.

The preacher decided to spend the night where they were so that he could have a long visit with this man. They talked a long time, and the sun was almost down. The rest of the family was out swimming and enjoying the day. The hunter told the preacher that it was quite a long distance to Indiantown, "So you might as well sleep and start out in the morning; then you will arrive about midday." The preacher and the hunter talked way into the night. The missionary learned many things about how to meet the people. The hunter advised that when they approached near the village to camp out about a mile away and let the people come to him. "Will they come?" the missionary asked. "Don't worry. They'll be there," the hunter said and laughed. He advised them on what to expect and reiterated to always talk Creek and hold out his hand to shake. He said, "They all speak Creek, except for a few." The preacher told the hunter that he was real glad he had met and talked with him and asked, "When are you coming home?" He replied, "Not for three more days. I need more gator and coon hides. Then I'll kill a deer before I come home, and I will bring you the meat.

"Ask for my uncle when someone comes around. Again, it might be him who will come to you first. My uncle is a medicine man and leader of the camp. He speaks for all of us. Also, there will be two older men; they are his brothers, but they do not talk Creek. There will be chickees when you cross the big river, so slow down and find a good place to stop for camping."

They started off again. They traveled past the noon hour; when they came upon the big river, they knew that they were near the little town. Slowly, they crept along. At a distance they saw the tops of the chickees of the Indian camp with houses of the settlers nearby. The preacher recalled the hunter saying, "Warn him. My uncle is a kind man but do not make him mad. He is a Snake clan man," and he laughed and said, "He sure lives up to it!"

"Well," said the preacher, "we're getting close. We're about a mile away. Let's stop over here where the trees are, so we can get shade." So they stopped, and everyone got out and began to make camp. They tied the oxen and horse to a tree, so they could eat grass. The sun was going down pretty fast, so they hurried up and put the tent up and started the fire to cook the *meal. But nothing happened that evening. No one came around. One of the children asked, "Do you think that they saw us?" "Oh yes," said their father, "They know we are here." They all retired for the night.*

The next morning, one of the women woke up to see a man standing nearby. She started yelling, waking everyone in the camp. The preacher went over to the man, extended his hand, and greeted him. "Helth'ghe," the man replied. They sat down on a log, but the newcomer left without saying too much. "I think," the preacher said, "that this was the medicine man that we were warned about. I told him who I was and why we were here, but he left without telling me who he was. We'll wait and see. In the meantime, let's get settled and clear the area for the camp, because I expect to remain here for the next three months or so. He told me we can get water from the settler's house."

Everyone started clearing the area, cutting weeds, building a fireplace, and fixing things around in the camp. Of the Indians, the preacher thought, "Maybe these people will help us to build palmetto houses when we become friends. Until then this will be our home." The missionaries settled in and waited for what would happen. How would they be treated by these Florida Indians? They went to bed early that night. No visitors came the next day. The preacher was uneasy. He walked down the road but saw no one except a few white people.

The next morning, their third day, one of the ladies got up early to start a fire. She looked around and started yelling, waking the others. "Look! Look!" A large can of flour was scattered around. It circled all of the camp. The rice was thrown the same way. (Katie Smith, my future mother-in-law, told me that encircling an area in this manner meant "We don't want you here!") Beans and sugar were everywhere. The only things left were the canned goods.

After standing awhile, the preacher sat down on a log and said, "Praise God, these people know that we are here! Thank you God. Ladies, fix what little food is left." While they were eating, he told them, "Act like nothing has happened. Just clean up and do whatever needs to be done."

At midday, someone looked, and there sat a man on a log. It was the same man that had come the first day. The preacher greeted him, shook his hand,

and took a seat beside him. The man was looking at the ladies cleaning up. "Cleaning up?" he asked. "Yes," said the preacher, "We are trying." No one said anything about the vandalism, as the preacher knew that this man knew what had happened. "You plan to stay long?" "Yes," said the preacher. "I told my people that I will stay three months. I am here with good news to tell. I will tell you all about it if you wish to hear me when you have the time." The man smiled and said, "Some other time. Later, later." With those words, he left.

The rest of the missionaries rushed over to the preacher. "What did he say?" they asked. "Nothing," the preacher replied. "He never said a word." "Did he see?" they asked. "He knew before he arrived" was the preacher's retort.

That evening, as the sun was going down, the missionaries had gathered and were sitting around talking about what they were going to do with no food. But the preacher told them, "Don't worry. There is a reason this happened, and God knows all about it."

The sun went down, and it was almost dark, when three figures appeared coming toward them. Some of the missionaries got scared. The preacher told them to sit still. As the men came near the log where the preacher sat, they set down bags in front of him. Without speaking, two of the men left. The third man was the one who had visited their camp earlier. He stayed and talked a few minutes, then said, gesturing toward the bags, "This is for you." As he turned to leave, the preacher said, "Matoe," "Thank you."

When the man was gone, the preacher got up and looked in the bags and found cornmeal, flour, and whole corn to make sofki (corn soup more often made of ground corn). Another bag had roasted garfish, dried meat, and a bag of coffee. With tears in his eyes, the preacher called the missionaries over and told them, "Never lose your faith, the Lord known we are here."

Although this was the beginning of missionary work with the Seminoles, the venture could not be classified as a success. When Lorenzo D. Creel came to the Indiantown area in 1911 to investigate the Florida Seminoles' condition for the government, he noted, "This is the point where the native Baptist churches of Oklahoma sent their missionary family to open religious work. As they only saw a few Indians, 'not to exceed five or six in the two or three months spent here' they abandoned the work in despair and returned to Oklahoma" (Creel 1911:22; West 1999).

It seems that throughout West provides academic or "printed" sources to back-up or underscore Jumper's family/oral historys in an effort to make it more "acceptable" history — I like the way it goes back & forth btwn the two but not so much the underlying tone of West's work - the way in which it says - here is the history that proves the truth.

5

Outlaws, Missionaries, and Medicine Men at Indiantown

My family lived at Indiantown. They were some of the first Indians that the missionaries met back in 1907. It was my grandpa Jimmie Gopher (actually he was my grandmother's brother, but I always called him Grandpa) that Reverend Goat was warned about. It was also Grandpa who brought Reverend Goat the new supplies.

On December 7, 1911, one of my mother's brothers, De Soto Tiger, was killed by a settler, John Ashley. Ashley and his brothers would become the most notorious outlaws in Florida. It all began when a dredge cutting a canal between Lake Okeechobee and New River churned up De Soto Tiger's body on December 9, 1911.

It was my grandpa who told the authorities that the last person he had seen with De Soto Tiger was John Ashley.

When Jimmie Gopher last saw De Soto Tiger, he had a big bundle of otter hides. Some were his, and some belonged to the other hunters in his camp. He was taking the hides to Miami to sell. Ashley had asked if he could ride in De Soto's canoe as far as the dredge. Two days later, De Soto's body was found. His friends and relatives rushed off in their canoes to Ft. Lauderdale, where they suspected Ashley had taken the stolen cache of hides. But in Ft. Lauderdale they found that Ashley had taken the train south to Miami. When they reached Miami, they learned that Ashley had gotten a ride north with a man and two women who were driving to West Palm Beach (*Tampa Daily Times* 1912). The prime evidence was at Girtman Brothers' Trading Post on the Miami River. The large stack of hides, which were definitely the work of an Indian tanner, had brought Ashley $1,200 (Kersey 1975b:44).

Meanwhile, J. W. Strongheart, who was reported to be a Sioux Indian and a Harvard graduate working as an assistant Indian counselor in Oklahoma, arrived in Florida to investigate the crime. Strongheart provided information to the *Tampa Tribune*, which stated that "De Soto was related to Strongheart by marriage and was one of the most prosperous and intelligent of the Seminole Indians. He intended to go to Oklahoma in the spring to make his home." While this information has yet to be corroborated, Strongheart did suggest to the local authorities, in a special meeting of the Palm Beach County commissioners, that a reward be offered for the apprehension of De Soto Tiger's murderer. The commission then asked Governor Albert W. Gilchrist to offer a liberal reward (*Tampa Daily Times* 1912).

Until this time, John Ashley had a clean record. His parents and brothers lived in West Palm Beach. One brother ran a trading post in Hungry Land. The murder of De Soto Tiger, the subsequent sentencing of Ashley to hang (issued on April 10, 1915), and classic jailbreaks—during one jailbreak Ashley's eye was shot out—launched the sons in this family on a course of destruction. The saga ended on November 1, 1924. A trap was laid at the Sebastian River Bridge. The Ashley Gang was apprehended and killed, supposedly as they attempted to flee (*Miami Herald* 1915; Williams, 1996:34–36).

In 1915 Jimmie Gopher's wife (a Wildcat clanswoman and sister of Billy Stewart) died. In keeping with Seminole custom, he moved in with his own Snake clan, including his sister Mary Tiger, his niece Ada Tiger, and her unmarried brothers. Jimmie Gopher was a medicine man and a bundle carrier, and he had a high rank among the Seminoles. The men who carry the bundle are the most powerful spiritualists and are the leaders of the tribe. They are highly trained and are responsible for duties such as running the Green Corn Dance, making medicine, training boys to be men by conducting a "Boys' School" which taught traditions, and serving as judges.

The Oklahoma missionaries traveled to Indiantown again around 1914. Funds were difficult to come by, but they also visited in 1916 and 1918 (West 1999).

One of Mother's brothers, Nogofti Tiger (b. 1896), was around sixteen when he went to Oklahoma with the missionaries. He died there of pneumonia in 1914 (Seminole Agency, Florida 1977). Another brother, Young Tom (Shuda), died in 1919. The third brother, Wildcat, was around twenty-one years old when he died of tuberculosis, also in 1919. Mother buried him in the large woods between Indiantown and Okeechobee. (Grandmother's sister [Tom Tiger's other wife] Mollie was also buried there and later her daughter Hattie, who died while giving birth to Agnes Parker in 1924.)

Because there is no record of any other cases of TB among the Florida Seminoles at this time, the Tiger brothers most likely contracted the disease in Oklahoma, where it was prevalent in Native American communities. If so, and considering Strongheart's comments about De Soto Tiger, it appears that all of Mary Tiger's sons had connections with Oklahoma and the Oklahoma missionaries.

Since these men were my mother's clansmen, when they died it was she who inherited. They had owned cattle, and she received some seventy-five head from each brother. Mother also had hogs. There she was, running the largest herd of cattle owned by any Florida Seminole at that time and doing it single-handedly. She also had two or three milking cows and horses.

There were no fences in those days. Mother kept the cows ranging around a big hammock by feeding them corn there. Those cows stayed pretty close, knowing that they'd be fed. Mother rode a tan-and-white horse and had another stallion and a mare. She had two little "cow-chaser" dogs that she had trained herself. The dogs were her main "hands" that helped her cut and herd the cows. Grandmother drove a wagon pulled by steers [oxen], following Mother and the dogs with the corn.

Mother took the cows to town about twice a year to dip for ticks and flies. She also sold some at that time. She said that if it wasn't for those two dogs, she could never have done it. After dipping, Mother led the way back home, about seven to ten miles, with the two dogs in back nipping at the cattle.

Grandpa hunted otters and alligators and sold their fur and hides at Bower's Trading Post. Mother and Grandpa also worked in Joe Bower's orange grove and picked the fruit to ship to market. They also cut sugarcane at $1.50 a day and picked beans and tomatoes for farmers.

The Southern Baptist missionaries had not given up on converting the Florida Seminoles to Christianity. In December 1920 a special committee of men visited the Seminoles for the Home Mission Board in order "to investigate and make a report to you with recommendations concerning the opportunities for opening up mission work among the Seminoles."

They later reported: "In our investigation we remembered how long this tribe of Indians have been neglected by the Christian people of America. After spending two days with the Indians and conversing with their leaders, we found more readiness to receive the proposed missionary than we have found in some of our Western Missions. Also the few white men of the vicinity we interviewed assured us of their interest and good will towards such effort" (Southern Baptist Convention 1920:3,5).

In 1920, when the Oklahoma Creek Southern Baptist missionaries re-
turned to the Indiantown area, my grandpa turned from those old ways and
threw down his medicine bundle, which was never to touch the ground.
"This, I believe," he said, holding up a little black Bible, "is more powerful."
He told the missionary that he wanted to go to the pond, which wasn't far
away, to be baptized. Jimmie wanted to bury all of the dirt and to be clean
like Jesus. He said he didn't want to wait another day (Jumper 1985:14).
That was his "changing day."

An account of the first baptisms of the Oklahoma missionaries read:
"Rev. Martin Goat and Rev. Alfred Goat made a missionary tour
down there baptizing the first four converts. Rev. Martin Goat baptized Jim Gopher and Mishi [Missy] Tiger [the daughter of Mollie
and Tom Tiger] in St. Lucie River at Stuart, Fla." (*Miami Herald*
1945).

A week after Grandpa and Missie were baptized, Reverend Alfred Goat
baptized Grandmother and Mother at Indiantown "before sunrise at their
request" (Miami Herald 1945). [The period of time when the sun
comes up is very important in Seminole ceremonials; that must be
why Mary and Ada asked to be baptized then.]
 From that time on, Grandpa was constantly persecuted by the others, who
were always harping on how he lost his power and strength by disobeying his
Indian ways. The medicine men observed, "Christianity is white man's
teaching and books. It should not be taught among Indian people." If anyone
listened to the teachings, they were in serious trouble with the Indian leaders.

The missionaries from Oklahoma could come to Florida to teach
the Bible only when they were able to collect enough money from
donations and other sources to support their efforts among the
Florida Seminoles. So for the most part, the Snake clan family of
Mary Tiger and Jimmie Gopher had to practice their new Christian
faith by themselves. It must have been hard for Mary and Mollie's
daughters Ada and Missy. The girls were of marriageable age, but

because of their new religion, they were shunned by the other Seminoles.

My father was a French trapper and sugarcane cutter named Barton. (The only time I ever saw him was when I was about twelve years old. I ran from him.) There were two strikes against me when I was born April 27, 1923. First, I was a half-breed; second, I was born into a Christian family. I was brought into the world by "Sis" Savage [Elizabeth Yates (Mrs. William Henry) Savage], *a lady whose family had been in the Indian trade for many years. "Sis" not only helped my mother deliver me but gave me her name, Elizabeth, "Betty."*

"I don't know what my family would have done without the Savage family in those days. They watched over us when our own people wanted to do us kids harm. Before me, all half-breeds were killed as soon as they were born. None were as lucky as I, being born into a family that had received Christ.

But Sis Savage was worried about what the other Seminoles might do to Betty. The newborn was brought by her Seminole uncle, Dan Parker, to the home of Sis's daughter, Fannie Canada Savage. Fannie was eight months' pregnant with her daughter, Callie. Fannie's eldest daughter, Elsie Savage Page, "remembers Dan bringing [Betty] to the house to be nursed, and our mother acted as a wet nurse for her until Dan took her to a safe place. The year was 1923" (Clark 1999a, 1999b, 1999c).

The Seminoles believed that half-breeds were evil "Ho-la wa-gus!" (bad spirits) who could endanger the tribe and bring on bad spells. Other half-breed children had been killed by their grandmothers or aunts, who threw them in muddy rivers or canals to drown. Sometimes they carried babies way out in the wilds, where their crying could not be heard, and left them there to die or for the wild animals to eat them. I had a baby cousin who was drowned in Ft. Lauderdale just three years before I was born.

My mother-in-law, Katie Smith, told me that Eula Mae Fewell got pregnant by a white man. She lived at Annie Tommie's Panther clan camp at Ft. Lauderdale. Grandpa was afraid of what they would do with the baby. He started south to Ft. Lauderdale from Indiantown to pick that baby up. His nieces, Ada and Missie, were going to raise it, but he arrived too late. Annie had already killed it. Old Annie Tommie had taken that newborn, walked down to the boat landing on the north fork of New River, and thrown that baby into the water.

Grandpa was livid. He walked over to the cook fire where Old Annie was sitting, picked up an ax, and furiously lashed out at the logs at the fire, splitting them, scattering them, and causing sparks to fly everywhere. Everyone thought that he was going to kill Old Annie. "I should chop your head—but I'm not going to do it. I'm going to let you live to regret it!" Then he turned and left. He had planned to get that baby and bring it home to raise along with me, where we would be welcomed.

Always the other leaders kept sending word to my grandpa about how he lost his work and strength (that is, the following of people needing his medical/spiritual services and his power in making medicine) and how my family disobeyed Indian ways. They stayed away from me, though, because they were still scared of Grandpa. His words were still powerful, and maybe they thought he still had some of that strong medicine left, even though he was a Christian. They were afraid of bad medicine.

My brother, Howard, was born two and a half years later, also of a white father. Men led by medicine men old Billy Smith [Panther] and Billy Stewart [Wildcat] converged at the edge of our camp one afternoon. They called Grandpa to come to the edge of the camp. We were eating our dinner, and he called back to them, "I can hear you all. What do you want?"

My mother, knowing that they were up to no good, picked up my brother and took me by the hand, and we ran into the woods. She did not wait to listen or to see what they were going to do.

"We came here," said one of the medicine men, "to try and reason with you!"

"What could you say, since I have no words for you as I have said before! You all know my answer, 'Leave me and my family alone.'" He was very upset and angry as he knew that one of the men in the group had been present

when Old Annie drowned my newborn cousin in New River at Ft. Lauderdale because he was a half-breed.

Again they yelled at him. They told him that he must get rid of the two evil kids in his camp. "They are bad luck for our people! You must kill them or hand them over to us. You don't have to do anything yourself."

Grandpa was really mad but tried to control his temper. Again he asked them to leave, but they said they wouldn't until he promised to do as they asked. Grandpa got up and went to his chickee and got his rifle down from the eaves. He fired a shot in front of them. "Leave, now, or the next shot will be higher."

They ran to their Model A Ford truck that they had come in. As they left they yelled out, "You haven't heard the end yet." Again he shot, hitting the fender of the truck.

When they left, he turned around. There was my grandmother still sitting at the campfire boiling coffee. "Next time I won't miss," she heard him mumble under his breath. He asked where everyone had gone. "They all ran," she told him. Mother didn't return with us for two days.

Grandpa told Mother when we returned, "Maybe they'll quit coming around us," but they knew it wasn't the end as they said they'd be back.

It was almost a month later. They came back, but not by themselves. They brought the lawman with them. The sheriff said, "I hear you're shooting at people. Why?"

Didn't the lawman know why he shot at them? "This man no good. Want to kill babies," he replied.

The sheriff asked for the gun he had used. Grandpa got it out of the chickee and handed it to him. Again the lawman asked, "Why did you shoot at these men? These men don't kill babies."

But he didn't know the old men were full of hate; he just blamed my grandpa for using his firearm against them. My mother tried to explain. But it was no use. He told my grandpa to get in the car, because he was going to jail in Miami. Miami is over 100 miles away.

Grandpa kept saying, "Me done nothing," but the lawman answered, "Yes, you shot at these people, and that is not right. Now get in the car"

"Wait! Wait!" Grandpa said to the lawman.

"Now what?" said the sheriff.

In his broken English, my grandpa told the sheriff, "Make people leave this camp and not come back."

"Alright," he said. He turned to the men and said, "I want you all to leave now and don't come back to this camp as I promised Jimmy. OK fellows?"

Grandpa said to them, "Hurt babies, and I will shoot all of you. Hurt babies no good."

"OK, OK," said the sheriff. "If any of you come back, I will put you in jail too. Is that clear?" he asked the men.

"Yes," they replied.

"Leave now," he told them. "I am going to stop at the store, and I am going to tell the shopkeepers to call me if they see any one of you here at the camp. I will throw you all in jail for a year each!" He turned to my grandpa and said, "Let's go. They won't be back."

Grandpa yelled, "If when I get out and come back any harm is done to these kids, I will come after you all, one by one, and shoot you all. This is a promise."

For two weeks he stayed in jail in Miami. Then one day, the special commissioner of the Seminole Agency, Lucien A. Spencer, paid him a visit because he didn't understand why Grandpa was in jail. Grandpa tried very hard to explain the situation to Spencer, who understood the Seminole culture better than most people in those days. Spencer went to the authorities and explained, "This Indian man should not be in jail. He was protecting his family, and he didn't hurt anyone."

So Grandpa was let out, and Spencer took him to Dania Reservation to show him the land that had been set aside for the Seminole Reservation there. He said that it was big enough for Grandpa and his family and no people would be able to bother them again. He promised to send a truck for Grandpa and our family in one year if he could be ready to come.

Already in the reservation camp was Jimmy's niece [Rosalie], who had married into the Tommie [Huff] family. He visited her, then began the long trip home. He had no money, so he walked, following the train tracks

all the way north to West Palm Beach, then west on the old road to Indian-
town. It took him three days.

There must have been quite a discussion between my grandmother,
grandpa, and mother, but in a few months we were getting ready to move
from Indiantown to the Dania Reservation, where we kids would be safe.
Mother had disposed of the cattle. She sold most of them, then turned the rest
loose.

It was 1928, and I was only five, but I remember bits and pieces about
the move. My cousins, uncles, mother, and grandmother gathered every-
thing up: a box of chickens, two cats, and three dogs. Everything that was
under the chickees was coming to town and had to be put in boxes. I kept
asking why we were leaving, but all they told me was that we were going
far away to a new place.

A big truck came rolling up to Grandpa's chickee. All of the things were
put onto the truck. I had a dog "Jeep" that some white lady had given me
when I was a month old. I saw her on top of the boxes in the truck and
thought she was leaving me. I cried and cried. My grandmother told me that
she would be alright and that I would see her again as Grandpa was taking
her to the new place where we were going. Then the truck rolled out of sight.

I don't recall much else until we got off the train west of Dania. This
town is on the coast east of the reservation. After the train left us at the
Dania station, my mother and Aunt Missie started putting bundles on
their backs.

My cousin Mary Parker was my age, and my brother, Howard, and
Agnes Parker were around three. Mary and Agnes Parker had been or-
phaned when their mother, Hattie, died while giving birth to Agnes.
Hattie was Mollie and Tom Tiger's daughter. Her older, childless sister,
Missie, took the girls to raise.

We all started on the dirt road heading west. We walked and walked until
all of us were so hot. The sun was going down, and it hit us right in the face.
We stopped for a while and sat under a tree and drank water and sofki that
Mother and Aunt Missy were carrying in a little can. After a while we
started walking again.

And so a family was relocated to the safety of the federal reservation. However, despite their Mikasuki language, they were considered outsiders there and equated with the Muscogee Creeks. It did not help that they were Christian. And then there were their half-breed children, who were allowed to live but would always be scorned for their difference.

[Handwritten marginal notes:]

Why this?

Reader is not stupid and telling them in a condensed version

What Jumper has just told in story format does not make it any "truer" or more correct!

Also coming from an outsider it makes one ask "How do you know? Were you there to witness this?"

6

Big City Island

We arrived at a two-room house that was built along with ten little houses. Those houses had just one room with a long porch. It was really small for two families to stay in. I don't know how long we stayed there. Eventually some of the families built chickees to live in farther west because the houses were too small for the larger families to live in.

There was nothing but trees and palmetto bushes surrounding the two-story building which was the Seminole Agency. In this building the superintendent and his family lived upstairs and the government workers worked downstairs in offices. A little to the west was a small school building which faced west. To the north of that was a baseball field. Young and old alike played on this ballfield. On the east side of the school building was a water pipe for all to get their well water from and near that two tables with wash tubs on them for people to wash their clothes. On the tables were sticks to beat the clothes clean. Then there were two ropes strung up for clothes lines to dry the clothes.

All of our cooking was done outside the houses either in a cooking chickee or over an open fire. Several years later a sidewalk was built in front of the row of houses, and a road was made out to the dirt road that went to Davie (Jumper 1997a).

My mother and grandmother built two chickees near the rock pit just south of the present-day Mekusukey Church, and then we moved there. One of the largest dairies in the area was near the reservation. Due to a faulty survey, the house and outbuildings had been built on the reservation property in the early 1920s (Stranahan Papers 1924). *When the dairy closed, my family was told that they could move to one of the houses. It was big, with three bedrooms and a porch.*

Later, the government tore the house down, and we moved out to a tent and a chickee. The government then built us a smaller house with two large rooms and a closed-in porch. Years later, when I came back from school, we built on another room with a bathroom.

Dania Reservation was on the site of an old settlement called Big City Island. It had been a real island in the Everglades surrounded by water before the eastern Everglades had been drained in 1906. There were two other islands to the west, Pine Island and Long Key. These three islands had figured prominently in the Seminole wars. Seminoles had inhabited the islands as early as 1828 until around 1900, when everyone left. The lands had been surveyed for the Indians' reservation in 1898, but the executive order that made them a reservation did not come until 1911. By then the Indians had all left, and the land around the islands had been drained for ranches and fields (West 1989).

The first person we met at the reservation was Old Annie, Annie Jumper Tommie [Panther].

Old Annie was born in Horsehead Hammock in North Miami in 1856 during the Third Seminole War (1855–58). Her family later lived on Big City Island, where some of her children were born. This family eventually moved to their seasonal camp on New River, abandoning Big City Island. Later, Annie's mother, Mammy Jumper, moved the camp to the outskirts of Ft. Lauderdale on the north fork of New River at Broward Boulevard (near today's city police station).

That was the location where Jimmie Gopher had gone to bring back the half-white baby.

The city camp was a hub of Indian activity. But by October 1925 Mrs. Frank Stranahan, vice president of the Indian Committee of the Florida Federation of Women's Clubs, reported that Annie's camp, which was located on private property, was "for sale and any day they will be ordered to move" (Stranahan 1925). This was a situation that Stranahan had seen many times before. She had watched helplessly as her Indian acquaintances worked hard to clear a piece of land for their fields, only to have a white person come along and buy the land and tell them that they had to move on.

Since 1917, when the Indian men's hide market slumped due to World War I, Annie and her family had broken with tradition and had begun to pick crops for white farmers, sometimes on land they had previously farmed themselves. But by 1926 her efforts to keep her family together in the Ft. Lauderdale camp were in vain. Her family, which comprised the last Seminole camp within the city limits, had been targeted. "The citizens and the city government are insisting that the Indians should be moved away from Lauderdale at once, claiming that their camp is unsanitary and they don't want the Indians located there in the town," wrote the assistant secretary of the Department of the Interior to the attorney general of the United States (Edwards 1926:2).

In 1926 the government was preparing to move the Seminole agency from Ft. Myers to Dania, Florida, on the site of Big City Island, and open a reservation. It would seem that Annie's camp was an important consideration in this major move. For Lucien A. Spencer, the special commissioner in charge, visited the future site of the Dania Reservation on March 30 of that year "for the purpose of selecting a site for proposed camp for sick and indigent Indians and a location for the Ft. Lauderdale camp to move to" (Spencer 1926).

The Stranahans had been close friends of the Tommie family since the days of the trading post in the 1890s. Concerning this significant move to the reservation, Mr. Stranahan talked to Annie's son, Tony Tommie, because he spoke good English and understood what Mr. Stranahan was saying. Stranahan told Tommie that his family could move to the reservation where land had been saved for them. On the appointed day, Mrs. Stranahan pulled up in her car, and Annie and her brother and other relatives got in to look at where they would be living. Annie's was the first family to move to the reservation.

Annie was a medicine woman, which gave her great influence among her people. It was the Seminole women who were dominant in the matrilineal society. It is significant that it was Annie's decision, as head of her camp, that resulted in the populating of the Dania Reservation.

Following Annie's move to the reservation, the Fewell family arrived, then the Huff family and the Jumpers. About thirty-five to forty people were living there when our family arrived.

The other Indians who would not come onto the reservation to live fussed because all of these people were coming to the reservation land, and some, like my family, were coming from far away. Medicine men came and said that we were wrong in coming to this government land—that we were breaking the Indian traditions. They also said we might be sold out and sent west, as others had been during the Seminole wars.

Katie Jumper Smith told me that Tony Tommie used to yell back at them. He told them to say what they wanted, but the government wouldn't send them out west! He knew this, I suppose, because he had been educated at schools and was the only Seminole at this time who had ever dealt with the government. He knew that they wouldn't send us away. He laughed at them and made them very mad. Then Tony told them to leave or he would get the government men to get the marshal. This made them leave.

Several years after we arrived, Jack Osceola's parents moved in. They were the sixth family to move to Big City. Minnie Doctor's family was seventh. Later in the 1940s, the Motlows and others came. In the mid-

1940s Bill Osceola arrived, and by the end of the 1940s his mother, Mary Motlow Osceola, had joined him. As in traditional camping situations, families stayed with their clan relatives. If sons came to the reservation, they would stay with their mother's people.

Grandpa continued to practice medicine and see patients after his conversion to Christianity. Mother also had medical knowledge, which she had learned from her father, Tom Tiger. However, many times I went with her to deliver babies, and many times the babies died. It appeared to me that there was something that she didn't know, because it seemed that they choked on something in their throats like phlegm. Mother apparently did not know how to clear out their throats, and they choked to death. I watched perfectly healthy babies die when they shouldn't have. I believe that is when I decided to make things better for my people.

Conditions were different on this reservation in fast-growing South Florida, and we had to learn a different way of living. Where we had been fairly well off in Indiantown with our livestock, on the Dania Reservation we were poor. We nearly starved!

Shortly after we arrived at Big City, my mother bought a new Model T Ford for $400—money she made from the sale of her cattle. She drove the car when she went back and forth to Indiantown to get us meat. When she ran out of money, she would go up there with Grandpa or Missy and kill a cow or pig that she had turned loose on the range when she left. She didn't have ice, so she would barbeque it, cut it with a big old knife, dry it on a clothesline, and smoke it.

Just as Old Annie had done years before us at Dania Reservation, we started to work picking vegetables for farmers and bringing the produce home to eat. We picked tomatoes and beans for J. D. Doane's farm on Stirling Road. We picked oranges at John McMann's Hollywood Groves in Davie. We also fished a lot in the canals that had been dug to drain the Everglades.

The reservation began to offer night school classes. My grandpa wrote about a fishing trip for his night school class in 1936. "I went fishing yesterday. Mr. King [the minister] took me to a canal 15 miles west of the Agency. We caught four garfish, two mullet, one catfish, and plenty of others. Two big fish broke our lines and got away. We lost two fishhooks.

"Many other people were fishing too. We saw tracks of deer. "We brought home plenty of fish. I had fish for supper" (Ft. Lauderdale Daily News 1936f).

It was a good thing that my grandmother had a lot of chickens. We had eggs and chicken meat, fish and wild birds, and pork and beef, when Mother went to Indiantown to get it. She also hunted gopher turtles. My whole family taught us kids that if we didn't work, we wouldn't eat. My grandpa Jimmie cleaned the agency house yard for forty-five dollars a month. All of my uncles and aunts were workers in the fields. My brother and I were put out in the vegetable fields picking tomatoes, beans, peas, and potatoes at an early age. We were paid twenty-five cents a hamper. Sometimes we'd make fifty cents to three dollars.

My grandmother made us save in three ways every week. If we got $1.50, she made us pay fifty cents for cloth to make a new dress, fifty cents for crackers, candy bars, and things like that for the next week, and fifty cents to go to the show in Ft. Lauderdale on Saturday.

My mother would take us and drop us off at the show. The admission was ten cents, drink five cents, popcorn five cents. After the show we got ready to go to Mrs. Stranahan's house.

We got a hot dog for ten cents, a drink for five cents, and maybe candy. We would stay at Mrs. Stranahan's all night, sleeping in her living room. She would get us up early and feed us oatmeal. Then she would teach us Sunday school, and we would go home to the reservation.

The men also hunted for the hides of alligators and the furs of racoons and otters to sell. Later, my mother learned from Old Annie how to make dolls out of palmetto fiber, baskets out of sweetgrass, and to make beadwork for the tourist market. They cut the palmetto fiber and picked the grass where the recreation complex is located today. They sold their crafts at Willie Jumper's grocery stand on the reservation at Highway 441, State Road 7 (across from Ludwig's Market today). These were the first commercial crafts sold on the reservation.

The Snake clan immigrants had become pioneering participants in reservation life. They had endured initial hardships and found an economic niche in making and marketing Seminole crafts that would provide them with significant supplementary income while allowing them to maintain a strong sense of cultural identity.

7

Our Seminole Ways

I remember the days when I used to see the old people sit around the camp-fires. The campfire consisted of large logs and four dead oak logs burning in the middle. That was where all women cooked the family's meals. Early in the morning before the sun rose, the older men started the fires so the ladies could cook. The men usually put on the coffee first, and they drank it while the meal was being cooked.

At noontime most of the men were out either hunting or working, so the women and kids ate leftovers such as meat, bread, biscuits, and coffee. The evening meal was eaten before the sun went down.

Children between five and seven years of age were taught to fetch water, sofki, and coffee for guests and to ask them to sit down. A child's first task was to learn how to cook.

The main food was swamp cabbage. The cabbage palm was chopped down in order to get the heart of the palm. It was brought back to camp, put in a big pot with a small amount of water, covered, and simmered for an hour or so. Honey and pork grease were added for flavor.

Many Indians were scared to eat turkey, thinking its spirit was bad and it would make you sick. Some Indians who do eat turkey will get the medicine man to doctor over the turkey before it's ready to cook and eat. That would assure that they wouldn't get sick from eating it.

Many Seminoles survived on garfish, for there were many in canals and ponds. This fish can keep for days if it is hung in a chickee.

Water turtles were also meat for Indians. Turtles were roasted by a campfire—turned until they were cooked. Then they were broken open, and the meat was spread on palm leaves. Some turtles were put in soup. The land turtles, called gophers, have to be dug out of a deep hole that they dig in the sand. The gopher has a better taste than water turtles.

Alligator meat was also eaten by the Seminoles. They would slice on the side of the tail to get the best part. Seminoles also took their hides and sold them to the white people.

When the men went hunting for honey, they would carry with them an ax, matches, and a net to cover themselves with. When they found a tree with a honeybees' nest, they would build a fire in the direction where they wanted the tree to fall. They would then chop the tree down. After it fell, a man would cover himself and smoke the bees out of the hive. He got all of the honey, put it in a bucket, and took it back to the camp. Honey was used to sweeten cornbread, lemonade, and sour oranges. The women sometimes cooked taffy for the kids to pull apart and eat. Honey was the only sweetener.

Corn sofki is made out of dry corn. Women pound the corn in a hole carved out of a stump. Then the large kernels are cooked to make sofki, and the finely ground corn is used for grits and cornmeal. Sofki is cooked with water in a big pot. Certain tree roots, called cappie, were burned, and the ashes were mixed with water to flavor the sofki.

After the evening meal, children gathered around the campfire for the older people to tell them stories. That was the way that the young people were taught the rules of life and their clan's ways. Those rules were to be followed. Young people were taught never to talk back to the older people. They were told at a young age that their uncle would punish them with a whipping or they would be scratched on their arms or legs with a needle. You knew that they meant it. The needle is put with a cup of water on the edge of the table or chickee, and the stick lies there too. (The water allows *the needle to cut without ripping.) You have to go get whichever one they tell you to. It hurts more to walk and get it yourself, and you cry all the way to pick it up.*

During my early childhood I had a lonely life. It seemed that my closest friends were my dogs and cats, and a bunny that a white couple gave me. I taught them to get along with each other, which amazed the reservation visitors who stopped by our camp. I could easily relate to my grandmother's stories about talking animals, such as the mischievous rabbit. Nights under the mosquito net in my grandmother's chickee and days in the field picking tomatoes also gave me plenty of time to hear the oral history and legends of our tribe and clan. The old folks used to say:

- *When you hear a red bird sing near you, it's a sign you're going to have a visitor from far away.*
- *Never put a ring on your pointing finger or thumbs—they'll never bend again.*
- *If a bear is killed to eat, when it is cooked never put salt on it. It is believed that if you do, when you go into the woods, it will kill you.*
- *If you are out in the Everglades and hear a woman cry at a distance, don't answer or try to go out to see what the problem is, because the cry is a panther, trying to lure you out to kill you.*
- *When there are lots of mosquitoes, a fire is built in the yard near camp and also under chickees. Lots of leaves are thrown on the fires to make smoke and drive the mosquitoes away.*
- *Don't ever wear feathers of birds around your head or carry them, because your neck will turn and you can't get it straight again, until the medicine man puts medicine on it.*
- *Bear's claws or bones cannot be worn unless first doctored by the medicine man.*
- *Books belonged to white peoples—not Indians—and you never look at them.*
- *When a baby was swinging in his or her swing, a little medicine bundle must be tied on the swing to keep away the evil spirits.*
- *Young people should never stare at older people or look at them or stand near them.*

· *When there's a strong rain and heavy thunder and lightning, don't move around—just sit still, or you might see a cut hand with a painted thumb under the table where you are sitting.*

In the old days, Indian women were never to talk to white people; so it was known at the store that all Indian women stayed in the back while the men ordered things for them.

When a girl had her first monthly period in her teens, she was doctored by medicine people to start her change of life. During her period she couldn't be around men or boys. She couldn't eat with other people, and she had her own plate and cup which she used. If she had to cook for the family, she put food on her plate before putting the food on the table for her family to eat. If she was married, she was not allowed to sleep with her husband until her period was over.

In the old days women would go a distance from camp where they had a shelter. There they would sleep, cook, and eat. At the end of a woman's period she would wash her bedding and clothes in a river or pond before rejoining her family. During her period she couldn't eat eggs because it was time for her to discharge her own eggs. She couldn't eat deer meat or wild birds. She couldn't go walking alone in the woods because some large animals would smell her blood and try to attack her.

People of the same clan can't marry. If they did in the old days, they used to get beaten and the woman was forced to marry someone of another clan who was the oldest man of the clan family.

When the mother and father of a young man see a nice woman, they go and talk to the parents of the girl and ask if their son would be able to marry her. If the parents agree, then the two would be able to get married. If a boy sees a girl that he likes, he would ask his parents to see her parents and ask if it would be okay with them if the two got married. Sometimes the boy and girl would like each other and would want to get married.

A mother used to tell her daughter that she should wait on her husband when she got married. She should cook for him and have the meal ready when he came home from work. If the husband was hunting or fishing, the woman should have his food ready early in the morning when he got up.

If the husband and wife didn't get along, if there was too much fighting, they had to part. If an Indian woman got upset with the man because he didn't work, didn't bring home food, or didn't care for his children, then the woman would discuss this with him. She would give him time to change. If matters got worse or they didn't change, the woman would gather up all of his clothes, bundle them up, and set them outside the chickee. This meant that it was time for him to leave. If he refused, then it was up to the brothers and uncles of the woman's clan to tell the man to leave.

After the husband left, it would be solely up to the brothers and uncles to help with the children and to help raise them. They would act as the male influence. If the men wished, the father could bring food to the camp for the kids. But his former wife would have nothing to do with him, even though he brought things to the children. He would place them on the table and leave.

When a man left a woman for any reason, the woman would take all his belongings to his mother's camp. Then she would go to the Indian doctor for a divorce.

When the sun was going down, all Indian mothers started counting their children and made them all sit under the chickee or on the logs by the camp-fire where she was cooking, as she had to account for where they were.

And so life went on slowly for Betty as the days unfolded in their prescribed manner according to time-honored customs.

8

A Childhood of Tears and Pranks

Life was not easy for my brother, Howard, and me as we faced discrimination from the other full-blood reservation children. I was ready to do battle with both white and Indian kids who dared to cross me or my little brother. "Many, many times my brother and I shed tears because we were half breeds. Indian children were unkind to us and called us all kinds of dirty names. . . I used to wonder where I belonged. If I was not an Indian or a white person, then where do my kind go? I used to ask myself this question all the time. . . The only playmates we had were our cousins and a few other children on the reservation who knew us well. The other children had nothing to do with us and were told to stay away from us" (Jumper 1985:5).

When Special Commissioner Spencer died unexpectedly from a heart attack in the Big Cypress in 1929, his assistant, John Marshall, took over as acting commissioner. Marshall was married to Spencer's daughter, who taught school on the reservation.

Whenever Howard and I or the other children would walk by the big agency house, the two Marshall boys would run out and yell, "Old dirty

Indians!" "Old black Indians!" while throwing rocks at us. "Where ya' goin',' old black Indians?" We would ignore them. But one day one yelled, "Kill those dirty Indians," and hit me with a rock. That's all I needed—to be hit and called names. I had been called so many hateful names all my young life. I had just had enough! I turned and went after the older boy, Spencer, who was stooping to get another rock. I grabbed him, and my cousins all ran back to help me.

It was a Saturday morning, and the boys' parents had left them home alone while they went shopping. We held Spencer, while his brother, Garland, ran back inside and locked himself in the agency house. I asked my cousins, "What should we do with Spencer?" One of us yelled, "Tie him up to a tree and build a fire under his feet!" My brother always carried a rope that he tied his billy goat up with.

Yelling didn't do Spencer any good as there was no one around. He cried and begged us to let him go. We all laughed and told him he should have thought about this before calling us names and throwing rocks at us every time we walked by! He pleaded with us that he would never do it again. We took him to our playground, where all of the trees grew thick. We tied him to a tree and sat swinging on the vines watching him. We teased him and said, "Get a stick and put it under him." We weren't going to put a fire under him, but we made believe that we would.

Then we heard a call from his parents. We told him that "you better not tell on us, and if we catch you again, we'll take you way out in the Everglades and tie you up where no one can find you!"

We ran toward the canal and jumped in the water and began to swim around and act like nothing happened. The boys' father got my grandpa and told him what happened, and our family started hunting us. Mother found us at the canal, "Where's the boy?" "What boy?" I answered. "My brother? He's over there playing on top of the sand pile with the other boys." She told us to get out of the water "right now!"

Meanwhile, Grandpa knew all of our haunts, and as he entered the woods, Spencer called out. He untied him and brought him out to the road, where his mother was crying. His father began questioning him: "Who did *this to you? Who did it?" But the boy said, "I don't remember who they were. I never saw them before. They must be new Indian kids. We were playing cowboys and Indians, and I was the cowboy," he told him.*

My mother brought us all back and stood us in front of the boy and his parents. Acting Commissioner Marshall pointed at us and asked, "Are these the kids that did this to you?" Spencer looked at us and said, "No!"

My grandpa told me years later that he knew we did it, but the boy wouldn't tell on us. Nonetheless, Grandpa let us have it with the needle on our arms and legs that night. He told us that if we ever did that again, he would scratch us harder. But those kids never treated us like that again.

My life was full of mischief. I was out doing something all day long. I could never sit around. Even at a young age, I felt it was a waste of time to be loafing. At times, I would go out and bring little animals in and tame them, such as squirrels, rabbits, and little birds. I even had turtles and little alligators in ponds that I made for them. One time, Eugene [Bowers] talked about bringing little alligators back to the camp to see who could get one on its back and put it to sleep. It was a kind of sport. Well, my gator never got out of the water, as I got hold of its tail and it turned around and bit me on my hand! I didn't know not to catch it by its tail.

Behind the Baptist Church was a pond with white sand. There were no houses or buildings, and we played there often, making sand castles with the white sand, caging little fish that we had caught in the canals. We called them cows and horses. Sometimes we would fish and build a fire and cook catfish.

We put ropes on old discarded tires and swung from them in the trees, rolled tires on the road, played hopscotch, jumped rope. There was no radio, no TV. Whatever we did, we usually kept at it for hours. In the summertime we would stay in the water most of the time. Our hair would turn yellow, and our skin would tan dark.

The commissioner gave all of us girls nanny goats and a billy goat to my brother, thinking that we would raise them to eat. But our people don't eat lamb chops or goat meat, so we just played with them. My brother taught the billy goat every trick he knew, and Billy would do it. When he said, "Run, run," Billy ran.

I had cats and dogs and my nanny goat. When I felt sad, they were there to help me forget my troubles. They seemed to understand when I talked to them. Many hours I sat crying and telling them all of my troubles.

One day, Superintendent Marshall's wife got after us and told us not to come around her house and yard anymore, because we were getting into her fruit trees too much. She made us very mad at her, but we left. The following weekend, we were playing on the road, when we saw the superintendent bring his family back home from church or somewhere. He got out of the car and went on to the house with his boys, but his wife was getting something out of the car in her fancy clothes. We were all looking at her.

Someone suggested to my brother to get his goat to tear her fancy dress. So my brother told Billy, "Billy, run!" The goat knew exactly what he meant, and went after her. This was to pay her back for the day she yelled at us. The goat bent down and hit her dress with his horns and started to tear it up and down. She went to the ground yelling. We didn't stick around to see what happened next, but as my brother was running, he called to the goat, and Billy came running and caught up with us.

The closest town to the Dania Reservation was Davie. It had ten to twelve houses and one little store, Anderson's Store. Stirling Road was known as Davie Road back then. It was a rock road that had been lightly paved. One or two cars might pass in the course of a day.

There was an old wagon near Mr. McMann's orange grove that a vegetable farmer had used. We used to push it up the hill where there was a sand dune. We'd jump on and ride it down. The farmer's son was our age, so he played with us, and there were two black girls who were the daughters of a worker there, so when we all got together, we all had fun with the wagon, pushing it up the hill and riding it down.

Another thing that we did was to climb up to the tops of trees and slide down on vines covered with berries. The berries were good to eat. One day, when our parents were out working in the fields, I climbed to the top of one of the trees to slide down. I had done this many times before, but something went wrong. *I flipped over to land on my arm and broke it. We all got scared when I started yelling, "I hurt my arm!"*

My cousin ran to the government office and told the superintendent. He came in the truck and put me in it and took me to Hollywood's county doctor, the only one in town! That was the first time I ever saw a white doctor. The doctor told me it was broken. I was scared to death, thinking he was going to cut it off! But instead, he put two small boards on each side and wrapped it. He said to keep it wrapped for three months.

There were four government horses that were kept on the [Hollywood] *Reservation to ride around and check the fences and property. My cousin and I decided to ride one day, so we got the rope and got the horses, and fixed the rope around their noses and got on them. Instead of just walking them, we hit them and made them run. I fell off, but the rope I had wound around my hand held, and I was pulled across the field about a quarter of a mile to the other side. When someone suggested riding again, I told them, "No more for me!"*

Huckleberries used to be everywhere in the woods in the spring. Our family would pick them to sell to the people in the cities for pies and cakes. We sold them for twenty-five cents a quart.

Once we got into a white man's watermelon field when we were supposed to be picking huckleberries. Everyone got a melon, and we were walking off. Then we heard a gun go off. You should have seen us run! One of the boys fell on top of his melon and burst it all over. In later years I learned that the farmer saw us in his field and shot up in the air to scare us. It sure did! We all thought we were going to get hit. It cured us from stealing watermelons.

One time my mother went to fix Indian medicine for some woman on the Tamiami Trail who was sick. I went along because I knew a girl at a camp there, and I thought it was a good time to visit with her. After being there about an hour or so, my friend saw her brother coming down the Tamiami Canal. "Oh," she said, "let's go meet him. Do you want to come with me in the canoe, or do you want to take the other? Do you know how to pole a canoe?"

I said, "Of course!" knowing full well that I did not know anything about riding in a canoe, let alone guiding it. But for nothing in the world would I have admitted that I didn't know how! So she got in one, and I got in the other. We were going to go meet her brother, who was coming down the canal. I saw her pick up a long pole to push the canoe and make it go.

She made it look so easy that I did what she did. But I pushed the pole so hard against the muddy bottom that it stuck in the mud. I hung on to the pole, while the canoe went out from under me, and I and the pole landed in the middle of the canal! It was a cold day, and I also did not know how to swim. My friend saw that I was in trouble. She pushed her canoe back to me, and I hung on to it and got out of the water. It was a good thing that the ladies had a fire going, because I had no extra clothing.

My friend said, "Why didn't you tell me you didn't know how?" Then her brother came up and said, "Isn't it a little too cool to swim?" I think my face was as red as a beet.

Brownie Tommie (Panther) was the brother of Old Annie [and lived in her camp where the Okalee Museum is today]. He always chased us off with scary tales of how ghosts or spirits were around at night. This had been going on a long time. One night we decided to scare him. One of the boys dressed like a ghost in white sheets we got off the superintendent's wife's wash line. We all waited behind the little clinic house [which was where the Bureau of Indian Affairs office is]. The boy who was dressed like the ghost hid behind a big tree, and we waited. Soon we heard Brownie Tommie coming, singing away, talking to trees and dogs. He was a funny guy when he had had a few drinks. He skipped and hopped, making funny noises. When he reached the place where the boy stood all in white, he kind of stopped, noticing something moving. The boy then jumped and yelled, "Oooh—ooh." You should have seen Brownie Tommie! He turned a flip. He tried to get up, but the ghost was near him. He crawled on his hands and knees, then finally got up and ran. He fell about two or three times before he reached his camp. We all got away, and we all laughed and laughed.

After that we never saw him around at night playing tricks on us. He *was a great believer in ghosts and spirits. The kids in that camp saw him gathering leaves, and he was using them the next morning. It's a belief of Seminoles that if you see ghosts, it means bad luck if you don't use Indian medicine. So that's what he was doing. We thought this was so funny and laughed about it for weeks.*

9

The Reservation School

Betty has related why her family came to the Dania Reservation, but the special commissioner, Lucien A. Spencer, had his own reason for advocating this move. He wanted more children on the reservation so he could boost attendance at his new school there (U.S. Department of the Interior 1927:8).

My brother and I, along with cousins and other children, attended the small one-room reservation school when we felt like it. The Indians believed that we had no need to attend school. It was the white man's way, not the Indians.' The school building was located where Howard Tommie's Smoke Shop is now. It was really us kids that were the reason a school was there at all.

Our first teacher was Mrs. Lena King, the missionary Willie King's wife. The grade level was first, regardless of our ages. The school was open for only four months in 1927 and for six months the next two years.

One time—I remember I was about eight years old then—Mrs. King made us girls white dresses to wear when we sang in some church. After she put them on all of us, and we were getting in the car ready to go sing, I got scared, thinking maybe she would take us off the reservation and never bring us back. I guess I was thinking of my grandmother's war stories. I started crying and jumped out of the car and ran toward the canal. My mother was fishing there about a mile away. As I ran, I fell in the mud. When I finally reached my mother, you should have seen my white dress!

"What's wrong?" my mother asked. I told her I got scared. She laughed and said I looked funny with mud all over my new white dress. She made me take it off, and she washed it in the canal! They left without me, but I wore the dress at another time.

Mr. Spencer's daughter, Mrs. John Marshall, was the teacher from 1928 to 1930. Another of our teachers was Miss Helena Higgens, who arrived in 1931. They all seemed mean, because we were not used to obeying or showing respect to white people. In all fairness, I guess they were pretty frustrated with us, and we really didn't want to have to learn things.

One time, our teacher Mrs. [Elsie] DeVeloe spanked my brother with a belt. He was such a skinny, bony boy that I didn't think he should be spanked with such force. I don't remember the reason he was getting spanked—he was usually good—but I came to his aid. The teacher had the door locked, but there was a window on the door. I broke it and opened the door and went in. I jumped at her with all the strength I had and took my brother from her, and we ran home.

Another time, I was playing outside the schoolhouse. The teacher told me to come in, but I wouldn't. She picked up sand and threw it in my face. I could hardly see all the way home because I had sand in my eyes. My mother was mad at her; she went and bawled her out and told her never to touch me again.

About three weeks later, we had some kind of party at the little school, and she was dressed fit to kill with fancy lace and such. Her hair was all fixed. In the kitchen there was a bucket. I picked it up and filled it up with water, then I went behind her and turned it all on top of her hair. I went around and faced her and said, "Sand in my eyes, water in your hair. We're even!" and left the party.

Despite such difficulties, life was generally good for Betty and the other children. As Christians, they were involved in religious activities on the reservation, especially when the new superintendent, now called the special commissioner, the Reverend James L. Glenn, and his wife arrived in 1931.

Glenn noted that there were 185 school-age students in the tribe (in all of South Florida), but only 15, or 8 percent, were receiving any instruction (U.S. Department of the Interior 1932:7). Interested in the children's education and welfare, he lengthened the school term to nine months, and the school was enlarged to include a kitchen and bathrooms. He frequently asked Betty and her cousins to accompany him to lectures. He would preach, and they would sing.

Glenn introduced Betty and her relatives to his audiences at clubs and churches around South Florida as Christian Seminoles who had learned the ways of the non-Indians. Today some might look on his attitude as patronizing and say that he exploited the children to make his own program look good. However, they were treated very well and enjoyed going places with him. "Mr. Glenn told of the customs and habits of the Seminole Indians [at the Woman's Club] and illustrated his remarks with implements and articles of clothing. At the conclusion of his talk, two Indian girls in colorful costumes sang native selections" (*St. Petersburg Times* 1935).

At the conclusion of these engagements, Betty recalled, "He bought us wonderful treats of food such as hamburger, steak and mashed potatoes, and ice cream!"

In 1933 some of the large city churches sent young women from teaching colleges to "needy or out of the way places as summer volunteers to conduct vacation Bible school, teach kindergarten, or do whatever seems to be needed in the situation," wrote Mary Lou Sanderson from Florida State College for Women. She and three other students were representing the Episcopal, Methodist, and Presbyterian churches to the Seminole reservation in Dania.

Sanderson described her students as follows: "Agnes and Mary Parker [are] eight and ten years old. Agnes, 'the tomboy,' is full of pep and mischief and Mary showing sign of growing into a beauty. Mary Tommie, 11, an only child, has a sweet disposition and a decided talent for art. Betty Mae Tiger, 13 [actually 12], is the natural leader of the group. She is full of life and in five minutes can think up more things to do than most children can in 20. Howard Tiger, her nine-year-old brother, is rather overshadowed by the four girls and makes little effort to stand out on his own" (*Miami Daily News* 1933).

At the beginning of the summer school day, one of the students held the flag while the other four students and the teacher saluted it. Next was health period. They went out to the camp pump to wash their faces. Then they lined up for toothbrush drill (and ate the toothpaste if the teacher wasn't looking!). Back in the classroom, they brushed out their wet hair and got ready for story hour.

"Five little chairs and one big one were then placed in a circle and each child picked out her favorite story book. Miss Bessie Hinson of Miami read them several stories that fitted the theme of the day's work and then they were free to choose some old favorites to be reread. Sometimes they told Miss Bessie an Indian story, arguing in Seminole over the details and trying to teach her a few Seminole words.

"Recess time sent us all out into the yard where we learned the Seminole game of 'wildcat and turkeys' and played the old favorites like Red Rover and London Bridge. Tag didn't seem to be popular," wrote Miss Sanderson.

Miss Merle Keel of Umatilla, Florida, rang a bell which began our music lesson. She led us children in singing "At the Cross," "Jesus Loves Me," "Revive Us Again," which we already knew and she taught us to sing "Onward Christian Soldiers." Miss Sanderson remarked, "They love to sing and catch onto a tune very quickly." (*Miami Daily News* 1933)

Often in the evening, the summer schoolteachers would walk over to the Tiger camp. Sometimes, around the fire, Ada Tiger would tell several Seminole stories while Betty would translate. One night, in order to make sure they had the story right, two of the teachers acted it out, hopping around the fire like "Rabbit" with a burning stick in their hand. Ada and Jimmie Gopher laughed and laughed.

Twice a week the girls lined up at the camp's shower house. With scissors they clipped the strings that tied their beads around their necks, took their soap and towels, and had a shower. While they toweled off and put their beads back on, Howard, the only boy in the group, took his shower (*Miami Daily News* 1933).

Community women under Mrs. Stranahan organized a Heromku Unokecku Camp Fire troop on September 10, 1935, on the reservation, Betty and her cousins joined. They were encouraged to compose news stories, which were written up and published in the *Ft. Lauderdale Daily News*, about the kinds of activities they were involved in at the school.

Mary Tommie wrote: "The girls made rest mats using wrapping paper and newspaper. Some of the girls drew pictures on their rest mats. The girls sit on their rest mats when they are sewing at home. On Wednesday, Thursday and Friday the Seminole boys made their rest mats, and then, when they are tired at school they lie on their rest mats."

Agnes Parker wrote about "Our School Garden": "We are making a garden at the Seminole Day School. We have planted peas, carrots, pumpkins, beans, onions, Irish potatoes. We still have more to plant—lettuce, cabbage, tomatoes, radishes and watermelon.

"When the vegetables are ready to eat we will cook them for school lunches. We like to work in our school garden."

Betty Mae Jumper wrote: "On September 26, the Heromku Unokecku Camp Fire group tore and braided rags for a rug. Two of the Seminole mothers helped with the work. They were Mrs. Katie Jumper and Mrs. Eula Fewell. Moses Jumper was also the helpful guest of the girls at this meeting. [Moses would be Betty Mae's future husband!]

"A guardian is furnishing the rags for the rug as it will be used in her home. The Camp Fire girls will earn a little money for making the rug" (*Ft. Lauderdale Daily News* 1935).

The year 1936 was an important and eventful one for the children in many ways. In March 1936, Howard, Juanita Fewell, Mary Tommie, Mary and Agnes Parker, Agnes Billie, and Betty presented a puppet show at Colee Hammock City Park in downtown Ft. Lauderdale. The play was the result of special First Aid lessons that they had taken from Jeanette Godcharles of Hollywood at the reservation school. Mrs. Stranahan, always the children's patron, was in charge of arrangements. The show was directed by Elsie DeVeloe, the schoolteacher.

The puppets were dressed as Seminoles. The students worked for weeks fixing the stage and making the puppets. The show was to illustrate experiences in which the puppets had many accidents with fire, drowning, and car wrecks. The children demonstrated first aid, sang, and talked for the puppets. They also presented a short program for the audience between acts. The new superintendent of the Seminole Agency, Francis S. Scott, was introduced to the Ft. Lauderdale community at this event (*Ft. Lauderdale Daily News* 1936a). Doubtless due to the efforts of Mrs. Stranahan, the show was written up not only in the *Ft. Lauderdale Daily News* but also in the *Ft. Myers News Press* and the *Jacksonville Times Union*!

At Easter time in 1936, the students from Seminole Indian Day School went to Dania Beach with the teacher for an Easter egg hunt. On this outing were Mary Tommie, Mrs. Tommie Billie (grandmother of Chairman James E. Billie) and Agnes, Jack Osceola, Willie Micco Tommie, Okay Tommie, Moses Jumper, Howard, and Betty. Jack Osceola and Howard won prizes for finding the most eggs (*Ft. Lauderdale Daily News* 1936b). Then they celebrated May Day with another beach party. They had lunch and swam and played in the sand.

The school had a Mother's Day celebration the week before Mother's Day. An article in the paper was compiled from their discussions during the conversational English period by Jack Osceola, third grade, and Howard Tiger and Moses Jumper, second grade. It discussed the school program and the school's attempts to interact with the parents and involve them in the children's newly learned activities.

> Sunday will be Mothers Day. Every day, when we prepare lunch we invite one of our mothers to come and help us. We cook and eat the lunch at the camp of the mother who helped us that day.
>
> On Monday we cooked and ate our lunch at Ada's camp. Ada Tiger baked bread-on-a-stick for us in her Dutch oven. We used wieners for sticks to wind the bread around. We ate tomatoes too.
>
> Tommie Billie helped us make huckleberry pancakes on Tuesday. We fried the cakes and ate our lunch at Tommie Billie's camp. We ate brown sugar and butter on our huckleberry pancakes.
>
> We are cooking and eating lunch at the homes this week so that our mothers will learn new things to cook.
>
> The Camp Fire Outdoor Book tells us how to cook good things. (*Ft. Lauderdale Daily News* 1936e)

It appeared that all was going well for the Seminole school. Certainly Mrs. Stranahan wanted to think so, but 1936 was its last year. It wasn't a success. As Betty noted, "We kids wouldn't go to school regularly, and our parents wouldn't make us go, so it closed because it was so expensive for the government to maintain."

10

Grandpa, the Church, and Traditions

Grandpa was content, now that our family was safe from physical harm. To his surprise, when we moved to the reservation, his boyhood friend Willie Jumper, Old Annie's brother, was already there. Willie had been Grandpa's "Dance Boss" when he used to run the Corn Dance. But Willie had also converted to Christianity, so they were very close (Jumper 1985:13–14).

Around 1933, Mrs. Stranahan provided a welcome service to her Seminole friends by organizing a Sunday school, with classes held every Sunday in the little schoolhouse. There were almost always visitors from the Ft. Lauderdale and Miami churches who brought clothes and food to the reservation Christians.

Grandpa and Willie Jumper both went to the little church across the road. Grandpa "couldn't read the little Black Book, but he carried it until his last day" (Jumper 1985:14). *Even when the congregation consisted of just the two of them, they would sit and sing on Wednesday nights and Sunday mornings and Sunday nights. My aunt and her two girls, Mary and*

Agnes, my cousin Charlotte, Katie Smith Jumper, and her two kids, Laura and Moses, all started going.

One of our teachers described our Sunday school on a Sunday in July: "There were 20 Indians present ranging in age from not quite a year old, to Annie Tommie somewhere in the eighties" (Miami Daily News *1933*).

In 1933 Howard and I went with our family to the first Indian gathering that we children had ever attended. It was the Green Corn Dance, the traditional Seminoles' major ceremony which lasts around four days. We went because Naha Tiger (Snake clan), the son of my grandmother's sister Mollie [Tom Tiger's other wife], *told us, as family members, to show up at the special meeting held at the Creek Green Corn Dance grounds near Lake Okeechobee.*

Some of the very medicine men who had hoped to kill me and Howard would be there, but their chance to put us away had long since past. Mother naturally continued to feel great animosity toward those men who had caused our family such fear and consternation. I recall her saying of Billy Smith in later years: "Now his own kinfolk's grandchildren are part white. I wish he was still alive. I would pull those children by their little hands in front of him and say, 'Kill them!'"

The Tigers went to this gathering because there were important issues to be discussed. The Creek speakers who lived near the lake did not have a reservation in their area. Two of Old Annie Tommie's sons, Sam and Jack Tommie, had married Creek girls. Sam Tommie wanted land for his family to live on a reservation like the one at Hollywood. They wanted it so badly that they were willing to ask the federal government, their old enemy, for land and other concessions.

They met with government officials from Washington, D.C., in April 1935. Harold L. Ickes, secretary of the interior, and John Collier, commissioner of Indian affairs, came to West Palm Beach to meet the Seminoles at the Seminole Sun Dance, an annual tourist event that many Indians attended. A petition was submitted to the government at that event by Billy Stewart, Charlie Cypress, Charlie Billie, Jimmie Gopher, and Willie Jumper through their spokesperson, Sam Tommie. Among the things that they asked for were for "all rights and privileges of citizens and a grant of 200,000 acres of land in the 'Glades" (*Miami Herald* 1935).

A few of the Indian people in Florida agreed with the plan, but most nonreservation Indians (the bulk of the population), both Creek and Mikasuki, were strongly opposed to the idea. Those in opposition felt that the small group of Indians who asked the government for aid at West Palm Beach were selling out, surrendering to the U.S. government 100 years after the Seminole wars by "signing a peace treaty" and jeopardizing the inalienable rights of the majority, who still considered themselves "unconquered" and in "a state of war" (*American Eagle* 1935; West 1998b:78).

The medicine man Ingraham Billie represented the large opposition group of nonreservation Mikasukis (*i:laponathli:*). He and his followers held this important meeting against the reservation people for many, many years. But in decades to come, this meeting with the government resulted in economic advantages on the reservations which even he was able to enjoy (West 1998b:90).

The Green Corn Dance, held in early June, was the time when all important matters for the tribe were discussed. Uncle Naha had asked us to come because there was to be a discussion about where they wanted the new reservation to be located. Then the government could begin to purchase the land.

Of course, I knew nothing about all this at the time. We were just kids, and while we were there at the Corn Dance, on the second day or so, we saw lots of kids playing and acting like grown people, dancing around the fire they built about a quarter mile from camp. It looked like lots of fun, so my cousins and I went to see what they were doing.

One of the boys yelled at us: "Look! White people! What are they doing here? No whites are allowed here! Look at that yellow hair." "A white man!" one exclaimed, pointing at my brother, whose hair was blond. That was all I needed to hear. Anger flared up inside me. I picked up a stick lying by the fire, and I hit that boy on top of the head before anyone knew what was going on. He went down.

Kids started yelling and crying: "She killed him! She killed him! He's dead!" People heard the yelling and came to see what had happened. My mother came running and saw I was the guilty one. Oh, she was mad! She yelled at me, "Go back to the camp!"

As I was leaving, I saw a woman bring a bucket of cold water and pour it on the boy, and he started moving around, so I knew he wasn't dead. I heard later from one of my cousins that he was up and running around.

There were too many things going on, so I didn't get punished, but I wasn't sorry a bit. I had been hurt so many times that I could have cared less what I did to them. I don't remember the end of the meeting or dance or when we left.

Life moved slowly on the reservation, but Betty did recall one disturbing event that upset the reservation community. A man named Johnny Billie (Panther) was accused by the still-active traditional Seminole council of killing Jesse Morgan in a drunken fight in the Big Cypress in 1935. Concerned that the traditional Indians would kill him for this alleged crime, Special Commissioner Glenn offered the protection of the reservation.

Betty recalled that Billie seemed like a nice fellow, and he convinced her Grandpa that he was innocent of murder. He eventually left the reservation, but then he beat up two women in Miami and was killed by the father of one of his victims (West 1998:33–40).

It was summer and hurricane season, which brought the worst weather that we Seminoles ever experienced. Grandpa Jimmie Gopher was in charge of preparing for the storm. Even though he was a Christian, he knew that our Indian medicine had to be made to combat these fierce storms.

The number four is important in Indian culture and medicine. You always do things in four. Like, if you take medicine, you take four sips. You always have four logs in the fire.

The first thing Grandpa did was to get four axes. One he got from the woodpile where he cut the wood. I don't know where he got the other three, but he got them. He jammed the handles into the ground so the blades were facing out in the direction that the wind would be coming. This, he said, would slow and turn the big wind away.

After he put the axes in the ground, he jumped up and went around whooping and yelling four times. This was a powerful chant to protect us. He also made a fire and blew smoke against the wind.

[When we lived in Indiantown], *I remember, the chickees were built so that the roofs could slide down on the corner poles and lie flat on the ground. When Indians knew the big wind* [ho-tale-tha-ko] *was coming, they would drop the chickee roof to the ground. Then the entire family would crawl under the roof and stay there until the storm passed. In all the years I have known, no Indian ever lost a life while being sheltered under a chickee roof.*

My family always seemed to know if the big wind was going to be strong or light. One time my mother said to me when I was about ten years old, "follow me," and I did.

She said, "you know the big wind is coming." I said I had heard the adults talking about it. She said she would tell me how to tell if the storm would be bad.

She pointed to the dark sky where the storm seemed to be coming from and she said, "we will stand here and you will know how strong the wind is going to be."

I stood with my mother a while and finally she pointed towards a bird way up in the sky. She said, "you see that bird high in the sky?" I said, "yes." She said, "well, that bird with the fork tail [the Man-o-War bird] is the one that will tell you how strong the wind is going to be."

"If that bird is flying low it means the wind will be real strong. When the bird is high, like this one, it means the wind isn't going to be strong."

She was right. That storm wasn't bad. She said this was how our people lived through the big winds. By looking at that bird, they knew if the winds would be strong or not (Jumper 1999).

The summer of 1936 was full of excitement for our family. Under the auspices of the Reverend Willie King, the Creek Indian Baptist missionary from Wetumka, Oklahoma, who had been working in Florida since 1922, a real church was to be dedicated on the Dania Reservation! My grandpa and Willie Jumper would be ordained deacons of our new church.

Reverend King learned to speak the Mikasuki language so he could bring the gospel to the Indians in South Florida living at Dania and Big Cypress Reservations and camps along the Tamiami Trail. He would be ordained pastor of the Seminole Baptist Church at Dania. Deacon Amos Marks, also from Oklahoma, who had been a missionary working with the Indians near Okeechobee, would be ordained a minister.

The church on the Hollywood Reservation was built by a contractor hired by the Southern Baptist Association. It was an unpainted frame building, with wood shavings on the floor, that would seat around 100 people. The church was dedicated June 7, 1936, during the time of the traditional people's four-day-long Green Corn Dance held in the southwestern Florida wilderness. It may be that Jimmie Gopher was consulted before the date of the dedication was set (*Collier County News* 1936).

The church dedication was at 3:00 P.M. Thirty-one Seminoles from Oklahoma, all dressed conservatively in dress shirts, trousers, and dresses, contrasted with the Florida Seminole women's colorful tribal clothes. The necks of the barefooted women were piled high with beads, and shiny silver bangles were pinned to their capes. Around 200 Florida Seminoles were there. There were eleven ordained ministers represented in the Oklahoma group, and many ministers and members of the local churches came out to the reservation for the church dedication. The Miami Baptist Association's ladies' league furnished a barbeque dinner.

There was a formal "ceremony of acceptance" for the new church presented by the Oklahoma Seminoles and described in the newspaper: "The barefooted women, brilliant in multicolored garments and yards and yards of beads, formed one line; the men, in khaki pants and cotton shirts, formed another. The men marched past the women and shook each one by the hand. Then the women marched past the men and shook them by the hand. While they marched they sang. 'The

Son of God died for us and shed His blood to save our sins,' they chanted in Creek." The ceremony ended in a square formation with the dignitaries in the center. The only white man to participate in this ceremony was Dr. C. M. Brittain, executive secretary of the Southern Baptist Missions in Florida, Jacksonville.

The Seminoles who came from Oklahoma were Mr. and Mrs. Arthur Wise, the Reverend Louis Harjo, Chitee Harjo, the Reverend Brown, Jackie Brown, the Reverend and Mrs. George Harjo, Eula Harjo, Billy Coon, Solomon Tmomokee, and Dave Walker. The Creeks were represented by the Reverend Roly Canard, principal chief; the Reverend Martin Goat, who had baptized Jimmie Gopher and Missy sixteen years earlier; Reverend Goat's daughter; and the Reverend Joe Culbert (*Miami Herald* 1936).

When the missionaries, reverends, and their families left Dania to go back to Oklahoma, my mother, my aunt with Mary and Agnes Parker, my cousin Charlotte, Katie Smith Jumper and her children, Laura and Moses, Howard, and I went with Grandpa, our new deacon. Willie Jumper stayed home to care for the church. We left in a school bus to attend a church meeting. I don't remember how long it took us to get there, but they took us to a church in Sasakwa, Oklahoma.

What a novelty we must have been! Barefooted Indians from Florida, the ladies with hairboards, beads, and patchwork clothes! This was the first of many, many trips I made to Oklahoma. We stayed with families from the church organizations there. They were interested in our clothes, and our ladies started making some Seminole clothes for them. Mother taught one lady how to make patchwork.

We stayed in a big old church with a big camp all around it. The congregation cooked and slept in the camp during meetings. The camp houses were made of boards with a porch in the front where there was a wood-burning or gas stove to cook on. These people were Christians, so we did not go to the Green Corn Dance when we were in Oklahoma.

Back home in Florida, Grandpa was harassed by some of the old traditional people who didn't like the new church. They didn't like the white man's religion. They told Grandpa to close the church! As always, they reminded him, "You were once a medicine man. How can you do this to your tribe?" They were really mad and threatened to dance all night against him and the church. If they danced all night against him, he wouldn't be around too long.

Grandpa looked at them and said: "My Jesus sees me. Whatever you do against me, he is my father and my trust is in his hands. Do what you want." Sure enough, the medicine men came to the church one day when Grandpa was praying. They walked around and around the church, burning bundles of herbs. They wanted to bring bad medicine on Grandpa and the church. Grandpa looked at them, then shouted to them: "That's all right. I'll pray for you, and my Lord will look at you as well!" They went away after that, and that was the last time they bothered the church at Dania.

1. Tom Tiger, Betty Mae Tiger Jumper's grandfather, ca. 1896. Photo by Charles Barney Cory. By permission of the Seminole/Miccosukee Photographic Archive, Ft. Lauderdale, William D. Boehmer Collection, no. 91.5P.15.

2. Florida Seminole women pose with Creek missionaries from Oklahoma, ca. 1912. Seated, *left to right*, Missie Tiger and Ada Tiger, Betty Mae Tiger Jumper's mother. Jimmie Gopher (Ada and Missie's uncle) stands with Oklahoma Seminole women. By permission of the Seminole Nation Historic Preservation Office, Seminole, Oklahoma.

3. The Snake clan's Indiantown camp with Oklahoma Creek missionaries, ca. 1917. The women, *left to right*, Mary Tustenuggee Tiger, widow of Tom Tiger; Tudie Tiger; and Ada Tiger. By permission of the Seminole/Miccosukee Photographic Archive, Ft. Lauderdale, no. 408.

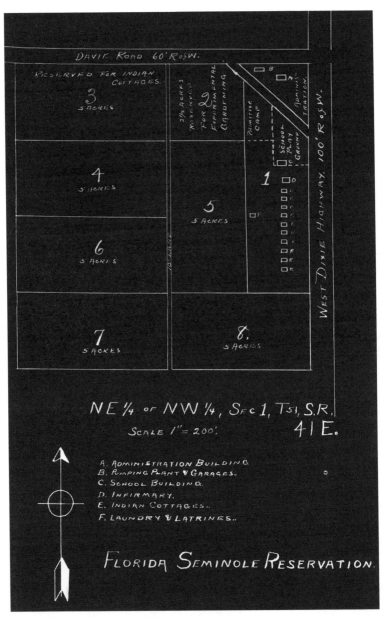

4. Official survey showing Dania Reservation improvements, ca. 1928. By permission of the Ft. Lauderdale Historical Society, Jane Kirkpatrick Collection.

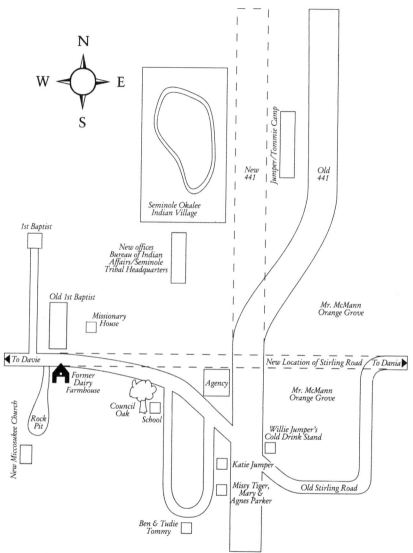

N

W — E

S

Seminole Okalee
Indian Village

Jumper/Tommie Camp

New
441

Old
441

1st Baptist

New offices
Bureau of Indian
Affairs/Seminole
Tribal Headquarters

Old 1st Baptist

Missionary
House

Mr. McMann
Orange Grove

◀ To Davie

New Location of Stirling Road   To Dania ▶

Former
Dairy
Farmhouse

Agency

Mr. McMann
Orange Grove

New Miccosukee Church

Rock
Pit

Council
Oak

School

Willie Jumper's
Cold Drink Stand

Katie Jumper

Missy Tiger,
Mary &
Agnes Parker

Old Stirling Road

Ben & Tudie
Tommy

5. Map of the Dania (later Hollywood) Reservation, 1928 to the 1960s, as recalled by
Betty Mae Jumper. Illustration by Scott Coventry.

Above: 6. Florida Seminole Agency headquarters Dania Reservation, 1930s, where Betty and her friends encountered the taunts of Acting Commissioner Marshall's children. By permission of the Seminole/Miccosukee Photographic Archive, Ft. Lauderdale, no. 456.

Left: 7. The Reverend Willie King, Oklahoma Creek missionary, his wife, Florence, and their daughter, Ruth, who came to work with the Florida Seminoles. Reverend King taught Betty and her cousins to sing hymns and gave Betty her first religious training. By permission of the Special Collections, P. K. Yonge Library of Florida History, University of Florida, Gainesville, Louis Capron Collection.

Above: 8. Schoolchildren at Dania, ca. 1933. *Left to right: (back row)*, Jack Osceola, Robert Osceola, Elsie DeVeloe, Mary (Charlotte) Tommie, Betty Mae Tiger, and Mary Parker; *(front row)*, George Storm, Moses Jumper, Howard Tiger, Agnes Parker, and Juanita Tiger. By permission of the Seminole/Miccosukee Photographic Archive, Ft. Lauderdale, Betty Mae Jumper Collection, no. 98.32.2.

Right: 9. Cousins Betty Mae Tiger and Mary Tommie, age fifteen. Photo by Ken Colyar. By permission of the *Ft. Lauderdale Free Press*. From the issue of November 19, 1936.

10. Participants and guests, many from Oklahoma, at the dedication of the Seminole Indian Baptist Church, Hollywood, Florida, 1938. Betty is seated in the middle to the right of the child. By permission of the Seminole/Miccosukee Photographic Archive, Ft. Lauderdale, Betty Mae Jumper Collection, no. 00.7.2.

11. Ft. Lauderdale Recreation Department's "Story Hour" for tourist children. Photo by the city's publicity bureau, January 18, 1937. *Left to right*, Mary Parker, Mary (Charlotte) Tommie, Betty Mae Tiger, Howard Tiger, and Agnes Parker sing hymns taught to them by the Oklahoma missionary Reverend Willie King. By permission of the Seminole/Miccosukee Photographic Archive, William D. Boehmer Collection, no. 91.5P.13.

12. Florida Seminole schoolchildren on their way to the Cherokee Boarding School in North Carolina, 1939. *Left to right*, Howard Tiger, Agnes Parker, Betty Mae Tiger, Moses Jumper, and George Huff (Storm) (kneeling). Photo by William D. Boehmer. By permission of the Seminole/Miccosukee Photographic Archive, William D. Boehmer Collection, no. 9–21.

Left: 13. "Instant portrait" of Betty Mae Tiger, ca. 1941. By permission of the Special Collections, P. K. Yonge Library of Florida History, University of Florida, Gainesville, Louis Capron Collection. Louis Capron had sent Betty some oranges and some spending money, she recalled, so she sent him this photo.

Below: 14. Postcard of the Seminole women's craft stand, Pippin Sightseeing Boat Landing, New River Canal, 1950s. The women, *left to right*, Tudie Tiger Tommie, Pocahontas Huff Jumper, Betty Mae Tiger Jumper, and Laura Mae Jumper. The children, *left to right*, Calvin Jumper, Daisy Jumper, and Pauline Jumper, holding "Big Shot" Moses Jumper, Jr. By permission of the Seminole/Miccosukee Photographic Archive, Ft. Lauderdale, no. 972.

Right: 15. Betty poses with her grandmother, Mary Tustenuggee Tiger, Dania Reservation, ca. 1945. By permission of the Seminole/Miccosukee Photographic Archive, Ft. Lauderdale, William D. Boehmer Collection, no. 91.5P.16.

Below: 16. Postcard, Kiowa Indian Hospital, Lawton, Oklahoma. By permission of the Seminole/Miccosukee Photographic Archive, Ft. Lauderdale, no. 00.8.1.

Left: 17. The first Florida Seminole high school graduates, Agnes Parker (*left*) and her cousin, Betty Mae Tiger, on the day they graduated from nursing school in 1945. They attended nursing school at the Kiowa Teaching Hospital in Lawton, Oklahoma. Betty would go home to Dania Reservation to work among the Florida Seminole and Miccosukee; Agnes would relocate to Colorado, where she married and remained. By permission of the Seminole/Miccosukee Photographic Archive, Ft. Lauderdale, William D. Boehmer Collection, no. 402.

Below: 18. Following World War II, Betty married Moses Jumper. He began work as an alligator wrestler at Captain Al Start's Jungle Queen Sightseeing Boat Tourist Attraction on New River. Photo from the 1950s. By permission of the Seminole/Miccosukee Photographic Archive, Ft. Lauderdale, Betty Mae Jumper Collection, no. 00.9.1.

19. The Seminole Tribe organized in 1957. The Tribal Council, ca. 1959, *left to right*, Frank Billie, Mike Osceola, John Cypress, John Josh, Billy Osceola (chairman), Laura Mae Osceola (secretary), Betty Mae Tiger Jumper, Charlotte (née Mary) Tommie Osceola, Howard Tiger. Photo by William D. Boehmer. By permission of the Seminole/Miccosukee Photographic Archive, Ft. Lauderdale, Willliam D. Boehmer Collection, no. 464–1.

20. Howard Tiger, who became president of the board of directors of the tribal business, the Seminole Tribe of Florida, Inc., ca. 1960. Photo by William D. Boehmer. By permission of the Seminole/Miccosukee Photographic Archive, Ft. Lauderdale, William D. Boehmer Collection, no. 518–96.

21. A tribal council barbecue and program, January 4, 1958. Betty Mae Jumper served as the emcee. Photo by William D. Boehmer. By permission of the Seminole/Miccosukee Photographic Archive, Ft. Lauderdale, William D. Boehmer Collection, no. 270–4.

22. A Broward County contest on the Hollywood Reservation selected those women who had shown the greatest improvement in housekeeping skills from July to October 1956. *Left to right*, Mrs. Barnes (judge); Mary Bowers (first place, a chest of drawers); Martha Osceola (second place, an electric percolator); Betty Mae Jumper (third place, a wool quilt); Mrs. Ivy Stranahan (Friends of the Seminoles); and Mrs. Clay (judge). The prizes were awarded by the Salvation Army. By permission of the Florida Photographic Collection, Tallahassee, no. 24121.

23. Aerial view of Dania Reservation. Seminole Indian Estates, in the foreground, was dedicated in the late 1950s. The older housing is on the left, the newer on the right. The Florida Turnpike (now the Ronald Reagan Turnpike), in the background, was allowed to cut across the reservation in the 1950s because the Seminoles were not organized enough to fight its construction. Photo by William D. Boehmer. By permission of the Seminole/Miccosukee Photographic Archive, Ft. Lauderdale, William D. Boehmer Collection, no. 00.10.1.

24. Betty Mae Jumper, manager of the Seminole Tribe's Seminole Okalee Indian Village in Hollywood, poses with a panther cub named Princess, ca. 1960. Photo by William D. Boehmer. By permission of the Seminole/Miccosukee Photographic Archive, Ft. Lauderdale, no. 439–5.

25. Betty and Alice Daye Osceola, a Miccosukee tribal member, pose with the first edition of their *Seminole Indian News*, October 1961. By permission of the Seminole/Miccosukee Photographic Archive, Ft. Lauderdale, no. 98.12.4.

New Tribal Council Chief Betty Mae Jumper (right) With Her Mother
Miami News May 9,1967

Squaw Now 'Big Chief'
Of Seminole Braves

By IAN GLASS
Reporter of The Miami News

OKALEE INDIAN VILLAGE — This may make Sitting Bull and Geronimo and other famous Indian chiefs of the past spin in their graves, but a squaw took over leadership of the once-fierce Seminole Indian tribe at 3 o'clock this morning.

Her name is Betty Mae Jumper, and she is a jolly, 44-year-old mother of three who looks like Bloody Mary in Rodgers and Hammerstein's "South Pacific."

Ten officials emerged from counting the votes registered at the Seminoles' three reservations — Big Cypress, Brighton, and Okalee, near Hollywood — after 4½ hours behind locked doors to announce Betty Mae had whipped her big, brave opponent Jack Micco for the post of chairman of the tribal council.

Her 240-pound husband, who rejoices in the name of Moses, whooped. "I knew she'd scalp him."

Tribal secretary Laura Mae Osceola, who was in charge of the counting apologized for the delay in tallying the votes (of nearly 1,000 Indians, 409 were registered to vote, but only 295 did). One of the officials, it turned out, didn't know how to count.

Betty Mae — first-ever Seminole, man or woman, to graduate from a high school — thus became the first woman ever to head the tribal council, which governs the three reservations.

The other big upset in the election, which is held

Continued on Page 6A, Col. 4

26. Ada Tiger and her daughter, Betty Mae Jumper, the newly elected and first chairwoman of the Seminole Tribe of Florida, are featured on the front page of the *Miami News*, May 9, 1967. By permission of the Seminole/Miccosukee Photographic Archive, Ft. Lauderdale, no. 98.12.3B.

27. Betty as Seminole chief on the cover of the Sunshine Magazine, *Miami Herald*. By permission of the Seminole/Miccosukee Photographic Archive, Ft. Lauderdale, no. 98.12.6.

Above: 28. Joe Dan Osceola, president of the Seminole tribal board, and Betty Mae Jumper, chairwoman of the Seminole Tribe of Florida, hold a new tribal flag designed and sewn by Charlotte Osceola. A contest had been held for women who wished to submit designs for the flag. By permission of the Seminole/Miccosukee Photographic Archive, Ft. Lauderdale, no. 977.

Right: 29. Betty with her lifelong friend Jean Abbey Winters of the Daughters of the American Revolution. Jean's mother, Erma Abbey, had enrolled and clothed Seminole children for the Cherokee Indian School. Photo by Patsy West. By permission of the Seminole/Miccosukee Photographic Archive, Ft. Lauderdale, no. 96.27.2.

30. Postcard of Betty Mae Jumper with her second book, *Legends of the Seminoles*, 1995. By permission of the Seminole/Miccosukee Photographic Archive, Ft. Lauderdale, Betty Mae Jumper Collection, no 97.20.3.

My Goal: To Go to School

In Sasakwa in 1936, I had met Juanita Tiger, who was my age. She showed me the first "funny" books I had ever seen in my life! We never had anything like that in school. She told me, "They talk to you!" She read me the funny books, and I really flipped out. She then told me to go to school. That's the way I would learn. So I made my mind up to go to school, so I could read like her.

The next year, 1937, when I was fourteen, some Christian people from Oklahoma came back to Florida to visit. When they left, they took me, Mary Parker, Agnes Parker, and Charlotte with them to attend Bacone Grade School.

I found it too hot in Oklahoma. Not enough of the sea breezes that we take for granted in Florida. We must have contemplated leaving several times. Charlotte recalled that we said, "Let's walk home," as we stood— barefooted and in our Seminole clothes—on a sandy highway. But we stopped and thought about it. We had no money, so we went back.

Not long afterward, however, the second week in July, the four of us started for home with Louis C. Brown and David Harjo. We got as far as Gulfport, Mississippi, when our escorts got so drunk that we got them to pull over by a police station. We went in and told the police that we refused to ride any farther with Mr. Brown because he was drunk! We called Mr. Brown's wife in Oklahoma and Mr. Scott, our superintendent at Dania Reservation. The officers put us up for the night, as comfortably as possible in a jail cell! Mr. Scott left instructions with the police that we were not to leave unless our driver was sober!

The next morning Mr. Brown came back sober, and we again headed out, but not until he paid a fine! I guess our driver was too scared to face Mr. Scott, because they dropped us off at the bus station in West Palm Beach and bought us tickets home to Ft. Lauderdale. On July 20, Mrs. Stranahan received a call from me at the bus station asking her to please pick us up and take us home (Pensacola Journal 1936; Ft. Lauderdale Daily News 1936b).

I had a mission when I arrived back in Dania in 1937—to go to school. I wanted an education like my friends in Oklahoma had. I wanted to be able to read funny books just like they did! When I returned home, the first thing I told my grandmother was that I wanted to go to school. She looked at me and said, "It's not for Indians, so quit thinking about it!" in a really mean tone of voice. I did not say any more to her about it, but I told my mother about it and she said, "We'll see." I also told my grandpa and he told the superintendent.

The government people tried to put me in Dania and Ft. Lauderdale schools, but the doors were closed to Indians. [Old Annie's son, Tony Tommie, and other Seminoles from her camp had been allowed to go to the Ft. Lauderdale school in 1915, but times had changed by 1937 (West 1998a).] *A black crop picker who worked in the fields with us suggested I might be able to go to school with her children, but the black principal in Dania said, "She's no colored girl. She can't go here!" I was really disappointed. I thought I would be getting on the bus to go to school at Dania just like the white kids did.*

The truth was that whites made a distinction between Seminoles and blacks and did not generally treat the two groups the same. While

Seminoles came to be unwelcome at lunch counters and restaurants in certain towns before integration, earlier in the century they had been welcomed on train coaches reserved for whites and admitted to the white wards of hospitals on the East Coast. They were also welcome in most white theaters and grandstands. The intent of the segregation law with regard to education was to place the whites and blacks in separate schools, not to discriminate against the small population of 700 Florida Seminoles.

The Seminole Agency superintendent, J. F. Scott, saw my disappointment and said, "I'm going to try to find you a school you can go to."

He got back with me and told me about a school far away: "This will mean that you will have to go away to school. It will be a boarding school, where you will stay about nine months out of the year and come home in summertime. Are you willing to do that?"

I told him I would go. He said that it would take a while to make the arrangements. All the rest of the summer I begged my mother to let me go to school. She at last agreed—I guess she got tired of me pestering her.

The months passed, and I almost forgot about going to school. It was winter, and I had been working in the fields picking beans and tomatoes with my grandmother. One day, I saw Mr. Scott walking across the field to where my mother was working. He began talking with her, but I didn't think anything of it, as many people came out and talked to us in the fields. But after work that evening my mother said to me: "If you still want to go to school, the superintendent said there are two schools open that you can go to, but both schools are far away; and if you want to go, you have to get ready in two weeks."

It was the third week in December, so this meant we had to be ready by the first week in January 1938. I couldn't wait to go and tell my cousin Mary Parker, who had half promised to go with me!

The next day I didn't go with my folks to work in the fields. I went to my cousin's house, one of those tiny government houses in the circle, and told her the news about going to school. I told her that we would have to go far away. At first she was hesitant, but finally she agreed to go. She also didn't go to the fields with her aunt that day but came with me to Mr. Scott's office to tell him that we wanted to go to school—wherever it was.

"There are two schools, as I told your mother," he said to us. "One is in Oklahoma, and one is in North Carolina. Which one do you want to go to? Both are boarding schools."

This didn't mean anything to us, as we didn't know anything at all about schools or school life, only that we would learn how to read and write. We told him we would like to go to the one in North Carolina, thinking that it was closer to home than Oklahoma. We also thought that because we didn't know the North Carolina Cherokee language we would learn English better there than in Oklahoma, where there were Creek speakers like us.

Our grandpa Jimmie, who was around the superintendent's office doing his job as caretaker, tried to explain what Mr. Scott was telling us about the school and how long we would have to stay away. We discussed these things with him and then told him to tell Mr. Scott we were ready. We also asked him to call Mrs. Stranahan and tell her that we were ready to go to school so she would get the clothes together for us as she had promised. Mrs. Stranahan, whom I mentioned before, had always been interested in our education. In 1934 she had started an organization of townspeople called the Friends of the Seminoles to raise money and the people's awareness of our needs. That organization, along with the Ft. Lauderdale Woman's Club, the Daughters of the American Revolution, other local organizations, and the government, would help us financially so we could go to school.

The following week Mrs. Stranahan came out to see us. She got us some used clothes and two new dresses and a pair of shoes each. Of course, we didn't know anything about what kind of dresses to wear to school, as we had only worn them once before! Some of the dresses we got for school felt so tight! I don't know how we looked in them. I remember that one dress I picked out was black with long sleeves. Black, of all colors! I don't know why I picked black, as it looked funny on me.

When my brother saw that I was really going, he started to cry, as he and I had never been apart before. We were always together. My mother said that we'd better take him along because he wouldn't know what to do after we left. So Mrs. Stranahan rushed him down to Dania, got his shoes and clothing, and he was ready to go. I never said anything to my grandmother all the time I was getting ready to go, but she knew, because my mother had told her that she had given me permission to go to school.

Even in the middle of our plans for school, we continued our participation in local events. In January 1937 we were featured in a program in Ft. Lauderdale. It was the first Children's Story Hour held in Stranahan park by the City Recreation Department for the winter tourist children. It drew 350 children and around 100 adults. The Ft. Lauderdale Daily News *wrote: "As an added feature a group of Seminole Indian children dressed in their tribal costumes and their many strings of gaudy beads, entertained with a group of Christian hymns and their theme song, 'Florida is the Land for Me' . . .It's the land of opportunity" (1937a). This song had more meaning for us now, as we would soon be leaving.*

With our Reverend Willie King, pastor of our new Seminole Indian Baptist Church, we attended other church meetings. One of the larger gatherings was at the Little River Baptist Church in North Miami. Thirty people from the reservation accompanied us. A facsimile of a chickee was made as the backdrop.

The *Miami Sun* (1937) announced the event: "Betty Mae Tiger, Mary Tommie, Agnes Parker, and Mary Parker will present a program of Scripture readings and songs in both languages. A vocal solo 'Saved by the Grace' will be rendered by Agnes Parker, who will sing and read scripture verse in the Seminole language and in English." Willie Jumper, the new deacon, was also in attendance. Reverend King, his wife, Lena, and daughter, Ruth, were to "sing in their native tongue."

At this event, the *Miami Sun* noted, "The last appearance of the four oldest girls on the reservation west of Dania will be the feature of the Sunday night service. Their further studies in music and other subjects will be continued at the Cherokee school located in North Carolina, a government institution."

Mrs. Stranahan told the *Ft. Lauderdale Daily News* (1937c): "The younger Seminoles today are desirous of learning the white man's ways. They are curious to know the customs of civilization and some of them are even more eager to receive an education than many of our white children."

We left on a cold day in a 1938 Chevrolet sedan that was used by the reservation's government office. I was fifteen, Mary Parker was fourteen, and my brother, Howard, was twelve. Mother and Grandpa saw us off. I've often wondered what my grandmother thought on that day . . .

Before I left for school, I had wanted to learn to care for babies, and I remember telling my mother as I left: "Maybe they will teach me how to save them when they are born. You always wished you knew how." My mother smiled at me because she knew that I really meant it.

12

Cherokee Boarding School

After what seemed an endless ride of two and a half days, on the third afternoon we reached North Carolina. In those days the roads were very narrow through the mountains. They would go straight down to the valley and then straight up again toward the top. When you looked out the window on a curve, it seemed as if the car would go over the cliff at any moment. It scared us to death! Most of the time, I had my eyes closed. I was sick to my stomach.

We didn't know where we were and thought the drive would never end. The driver finally stopped in front of a large building, the girls' building of the Quaker-operated Cherokee Indian Boarding School. He got out and went up the stairway to inquire where we were to go. An old white-headed lady came out to greet us. She was the matron, Juliette White, with whom I was to spend the next eight years. She told us to get our things and follow her to our room.

When we got ready to go with her into the building, my brother started crying, but she told him he had to go to the boys' building up the hill. "There will be lots of boys your size and age, and you will be okay there." My brother was only twelve years old, and the haircut my mother did on him before we left was like she had put a bowl on his head and cut around it. Later in the week, I noticed that someone had fixed it up for him.

So we girls went into our building and to the room where we were to sleep. I stood there looking around and wondered, "Why did I make such a fuss to come to school?" I already yearned to go home. To make things worse, they told us we had to sleep on the top bunk beds, as the bottoms were already taken by two Chitamacha girls from Louisiana. But we were all in the same boat, feeling very low, in a strange place, in a valley with high mountains sur-rounding us—where you can't see far away as you can at home.

Not long after we had put our things away, a bell rang. I asked the girls in the room, who had been sitting, watching us, "What's that?" One of them answered me, "It's the five o'clock bell to let the girls who are working in the kitchen or dining room know that it's time for them to go. The girls in the kitchen help with the cooking. The girls in the dining room set the tables and wait on the tables."

Then the 5:30 bell rang. That meant that we were to go downstairs and line up on the sidewalk to go to eat. We all marched down to the dining room, with the little girls in front. The boys did the same thing, coming down from their dormitory on the hill. I soon found out that all of us lived by this bell all day long!

The older girls were assigned to get the little girls ready to eat by washing their hands, for example. There was a girl assigned to us when we first came, to see that we adjusted to the rules and regulations. Minnie Ross, a Cherokee girl, came for us on that first day when the 5:30 bell rang and was with us in the dining room when we ate our first meal. She pointed us to some empty chairs and told us to stand until we all said a prayer.

Before we all sat down to eat, my brother came down with the little boys. Everyone turned to look at us. I didn't know it then, but the students made a habit of looking at new people when they came to school. I learned to do the same thing in later years. But on that first day, I reflected that at home I would have been punished for staring at a stranger. We could glance but never stare. That was one of the hardest things for me to adjust to at school. But that first evening, everyone stared at us. As we looked around, all eyes seemed to be on us, and my brother barely ate anything.

The next day seemed even worse. At the noon meal, there were about 200 students eating. The kids from day school came in on buses—loads of them. It was a very large dining room, and it held all of the young students and the high school students as well. I remember standing that day, waiting for prayer. I looked around and noticed a guy with the bluest eyes and black wavy hair staring back at me. My mind was saying, "What a funny-looking Indian!" Then I looked another way and saw a blond-haired girl. I thought, "Isn't this an 'Indian' school?" I later learned that some students had only a little Indian blood, while others were full-bloods. I thought to myself, "Never again will I ever ask where my kind belong!"

We lived with the stares and being with strangers for the next several weeks until they all got used to us. I learned how to live in a new world. I watched everything that they did and said. If I didn't understand, they would repeat it until I caught on. Our fourth-grade teacher taught us how to speak and read words with pictures.

Some students started calling us Gators or Crocodiles. This is when my brother got his nickname, Crockie. Some called us Cinnamon Rolls—a little alliteration on Seminoles. *At first, I really hated the name-calling. Then one day I thought to myself, "If I'm going to stay in this school, I'm going to have to play their game." So the next time a boy yelled at me, "Hi Gator! How's it with you?" I answered back, "Cool, but I'll get used to it!" It kind of surprised him, as for a long time I never said anything but smiled at them. Another time, one yelled at me, "Hi Cinnamon Roll!" and I turned and answered back, "Hi, I'm sweet—want to try me out?" You should have seen his face. He couldn't believe I said it. His buddy told him as they passed by, "Guess that will hold you for a while!"*

It was one of the students who had told me, "Get with it, girl. Talk back to them!" At last I had stood up for myself. They finally let up on us and left us alone, and we all became friends and a part of the school.

I learned the ropes and the school rules. Some of the hardest things for me to catch on or adjust to were in the girls' building. Little things, they seem now, like closing the doors quietly—I managed to slam the door every time I went in or out of my room. My matron called me down a few times; then one day she put my name on the board with four extra hours to work off on my own time. I flipped when I saw that! It's a real punishment because you had to work it off before you could go to a dance on Friday or a movie on Saturday. After school I started working it off. It took me all week, but I was done by Friday. The brass on every door in the hallway and the bathrooms was so clean, you could see yourself in it! The hallways were always shining as the girls were always working off their punishments there. I never wanted to see my name on the board again, so when I went in and out of my room, no one ever knew I was around from that day on. Like a mouse going in and out of its hole, I crept through the building.

After supper we could go down the hill for a while if we were not being punished, and if it was still daylight, but we had to be in at 7:00 to line up in the basement of the girls' building. When we lined up, the matron talked to us of many things, good and bad, and reminded us that we all must abide by the rules of the school. We all must learn to obey and follow regulations or we would be sent home. We had been given uniforms— yellow, blue, green shirtwaists with belts—and shoes. After receiving our daily lecture, we would all say the Lord's Prayer, then the little girls went straight to bed at 7:30. The bigger girls stayed up and did homework or other things that needed to be done before going to bed at 8:30. At 9:00 all lights went out.

The next bell rang at 6:00 A.M. for everyone to get up. Some girls worked in the kitchen, and some worked with the younger girls cleaning rooms and washing up. After breakfast, at 7:30 A.M., the girls all came back to their rooms and made their beds and got ready to go to school at 8:20 A.M. A total of about 300 boys and girls were in the boarding school.

By May, Mrs. Stranahan had gotten several letters from us. Mary Parker wrote: "Oh Mrs. Stranahan you don't know how glad we were to get dresses. We was run around and show the girls and Friday nite we all had a box supper and we wear these dresses and we were so glad to have it. Thank you very much" (Ft. Lauderdale Daily News 1937b).

One time, before I had learned often-used terms and the names of cleaners, I was put in the girls' dorm on detail to mop the hallways. "Put lots of elbow grease into it!" I was told. About an hour later, when I had finished mopping and was ready to shine the floors, I went downstairs to the cleaning supply room and started hunting the "elbow grease." Finally, I came back upstairs, where the matron was sitting. I told her, "I can't find the elbow grease." She started laughing and laughing! I stood there feeling like a dummy and couldn't understand why she was laughing. Then when she saw that I wasn't joking around, she quit laughing and began to explain to me what she had meant by putting "elbow grease" into the job. It meant "work hard on the floor and make it shine!" Well, I told her, "How would I know, when I was raised half of my life in a chickee with no walls or shiny floors. Give me some time, and I'll learn how the outside world turns!"

The foods that you grew up with seem really important when you are transplanted far away. My cousin Mary remembered that she missed sofki because we always had it at home. But for me, I missed lapalee, bread that my grandmother made in a big pan.

One night in the middle of winter, some girls told us it looked like it would snow. Sure enough, it snowed all through the night! I didn't know what snow was; at home the only snow I saw was the ice truck delivering ice to some of the houses on the reservation. Frank Tommie and Ben Tommie would buy a little ice and put it in a bucket of water to drink. We used to chase behind the ice truck to get pieces of ice.

Next morning, my cousin woke me up, telling me to look out the window. When I did, I saw a white sheet of snow covering the ground and trees. What a sight it was! Beautiful! My cousin and I ran out the front door and went down to touch it, barefoot! Miss White saw us out there and yelled at us, "Do you want to catch a cold or pneumonia?" She was mad at us. "Look at your feet! No shoes! What do you think you are? Polar bears!!"

I didn't realize I'd be seeing snow every winter for the next seven and a half years. That afternoon it came again. The ground was covered with white snow. The next day was Saturday, no school, so I sat by the window *in the living room and watched the snow falling from the sky. All afternoon I asked myself, "Where does it come from?"*

My new experiences in the following days were to learn to walk on snow and, when it melted and froze, to learn to walk without falling. I had to learn to adjust to the freezing wind that hit my face and figure out how to keep warm.

There was an outbreak of measles in December 1937. The other girls and I hoped that we wouldn't get them until after the Christmas holidays.

As the months rolled by, each season had its own beauty. When spring popped out, the snow all melted into the rivers and streams, while everything began to turn green in the mountains. All kinds of birds returned from the South, singing all kinds of tunes while hunting food and making nests. Beautiful flowers started peeping out and had their own way of adding to the beauty of the summer months. When we saw all these changes, we began to think and count the days until school would be out and we would be going home!

We were in the schoolroom for a half-day. The other half of the day we spent going to such classes as sewing, cooking, basket making, pottery making, and learning how to clean house and keep it clean. Some girls learned how to make crafts and bake bread and cakes. After lunch, between 12:30 and 1:00, we played records, and that's when some of us learned to dance— square dance and the jitterbug!

One-quarter day in the afternoon we did our chores. We worked in the kitchen, dining room, laundry, school building, or girls' dorm. The boys worked in the boys' dorm, cleaning halls and bathrooms. Some guys went to the dairy farm. They learned to milk cows and to take care of them. Some of them went to work on the school's farm learning to plant vegetables, and others attended mechanics' school, where they learned to fix cars. As the boys began to leave for war jobs or as they enlisted in the armed services, I began to drive a tractor for the school's farm program. Other girls hoed and planted beans and potatoes. The beans were put up in jars, and the potatoes were stored in the potato house. We ate them the rest of the school year.

On Friday nights there was square dancing and jitterbug dances. I worked Saturday mornings baby-sitting or cleaning at local people's homes for fifteen cents an hour. Also on weekends I would cook and wait on tables at the Employees' Club for teachers and school workers, which had a big dining room. Wednesday nights and Sunday mornings we went to Baptist Church services. Sunday afternoons, we went on a two-mile walk.

June 1938 to June 1945 was a long, rough, and windy road for me. I had to learn to speak English so people could understand what I was trying to say. Learning to read was also rough, as was spelling—I never thought I'd learn to spell. All in all, I learned how to cope with school life in the outside world. It was very different from what I was used to. Our days were full. If you really wanted to learn, it was all there for you to absorb.

Most of today's critics of the Indian boarding schools come down hard on the government's solution to the Indian Problem, which was geared toward acculturating the Indian students into mainstream society at the expense of their tribal culture. Since acculturation was Betty's personal goal, she was grateful for the opportunity to get an education.

By 1939 I was in the swing of things. I wrote Mrs. Stranahan: "Oh I do hope you can make arrangements about summer school so I can go. I want to finish seventh grade and get in eight if I can. Hope you can help me on that" (Jumper 1939).

The people who were the greatest influence in my life at school were Miss Juliette White, our matron, her sister Maude White, and my homeroom teacher, Miss Hollingsworth. They listened to me for hours and gave me wonderful practical advice I could use for the rest of my life. My best schoolmate was Lucinda Lambert, a Cherokee.

The two Marys—my cousin Mary Parker and Mary (Charlotte) Tommie—had left by 1939, but Mary's sister, Agnes Parker, had arrived. That year I joined the Baptist Youth group. There were fifty-seven of us girls when we started out, but with academics, attrition, and the approach of World War II, only six of us were left by graduation. We went on one annual outing on the school bus, to Asheville to shop for Christmas presents.

Every six weeks, classes changed; so did chores. When I first got there, I was put in the kitchen to help out. Then to the laundry, then to the girls' building, where I stayed most of the time, helping the little girls get dressed and do their lessons. I got them up in the morning, then took care of them after school, and I put them to bed at night. Some of us bigger girls had to keep an eye on the younger children all the time. They were to clean their rooms, take baths, get lined up, and go to their meals. This was my routine for the rest of my school days.

The Cherokee Indian Fair was an annual event, which I still attend when I can. In October 1940, several older men from the Seminole Tribe —Cuffney Tiger, Naha Tiger (my uncle), Charlie Micco, and Jimmie Billie—were invited for an official visit to the four-day-long fair. The fair featured Indian crops and craftswork in exhibits, demonstrations, and booths; an Indian choir singing contest, a spinning contest, a Cherokee Indian ball game, archery and blow gun contests, a baby show, square dances, and a carnival (Asheville Carolina Times 1940).

At Christmastime I always have memories from years ago when I was a small girl and didn't know what Christmas was about. One year I saw young white girls my age. They were carrying dolls. They said, "Santa gave them to us."

For the longest time I used to wonder who was this man Santa Claus who went around and handed out dolls to children and why didn't he come to me. I wondered how you ask Santa to give you a doll. But I never learned how to go about asking. Finally, I just figured you had to be white to get a doll, so that's that.

Years later, at Cherokee, my family didn't have any money so over the Christmas holidays I couldn't go home like the other kids. One day, I was out in the hall cleaning for my room and board, and two big boxes came to the girls' building. I called my matron. She came out and signed for the boxes.

"Oh," she said, "I wonder what's in these boxes."

She opened one large box, and what did I see? Nothing but dolls and dolls. They were gifts collected by local women and donated to our school for the young girls.

As I looked, I saw an old-fashioned doll that looked like a real baby. I picked it up and admired it. I was saying to myself, "Why couldn't something like this ever come in my day?"

The matron saw me and said, "You like that doll, don't you?" Then I told her my story of wanting a doll and never getting it in my life.

I laid the doll back in the box, but the matron picked it up and said, "Here, take it and wash her clothes and clean it up and put it on your bed."

I stood there thinking, "I'm too old for a doll" But the matron kept saying, "Take it. Take it."

That doll stayed on my pillow every day while I remained at Cherokee (Jumper 1998a).

I came to know Mrs. [Erma, Mrs. O. H.] Abbey in my first few years at school. She was a friend of Mrs. Stranahan's, and she began sending us things like oranges, clothes, and a little bit of money. At Christmas, she would send us some more clothes and money for winter shoes.

I learned that Mrs. Abbey was a member of Mrs. Stranahan's organization, the Friends of the Seminoles. She was also the head of the local chapter of the Daughters of the American Revolution in which Mrs. Stranahan was an active member. Mrs. Abbey would try to locate summer jobs for us when we came back home so that we could earn a little bit of extra money for necessities during the school year. I wrote Mrs. Abbey, "You have done alots for us. More than I can ever try to repay" (Jumper 1945b).

There was also a Mrs. Guinn, who worked for the Baptist Church in Miami. She often came out to the reservation. On one visit she told Mrs. Abbey that she had arranged for some of us to work in a big laundry in Miami. I stayed at her home, and George Storm, who was by then a student at Cherokee, stayed with his uncle at a tourist attraction in Miami.

From that time on, we had the help of both Mrs. Stranahan and Mrs. Abbey to prepare us to go back to school. Best of all, Mrs. Abbey had a daughter, Jean, who was just about my size. Jean used to give me some of her clothes to take back to school with me.

Mary Parker had quit school to come home and marry Joe Bowers. While home one summer around 1943, Mary and I and her baby, Eugene, went to McCrory's Five and Ten Cent Store. Although Indians had to go down an alley to the back of the store to order their food like the black people did, I decided that we should sit down at the counter and order a hamburger and a Coke. The waitress came over and said, "I can't serve you. You'll have to go to the back door."

Then the cook appeared and said gruffly, "You bastards get out. You're not welcome!"

I got really mad. I stood up and said to him, "I'm going to make you serve me!"

He cussed me out!

"In two weeks you'll serve me!" I threatened, as, shaking with anger, we headed to the door. I headed straight to Mrs. Stranahan's house. She took me directly to the mayor.

In two weeks, we showed up at McCrory's lunch counter. Mrs. Stranahan and the mayor told me to sit down, while they remained nearby. The cook came over and began to give me a hard time. Then the mayor stepped up with Mrs. Stranahan. The mayor said, "You start serving these Indians, or I'll close the store down!" The cook fixed the food and served it himself. But I didn't touch it; I just stood up and left! At this time, Seminoles were segregated in eating establishments, even in Dania.

Another summer, when I was about seventeen years old, we had a new superintendent, Mr. Marmon. He had gone to Miami for an operation, but when he returned to the agency at Dania, he began to have migraines. His wife told me, "He can't sleep." You could see that she was very tired too, from taking care of him. I picked bay leaves for medicine and put them in a small bag. I told her to burn them in the evening and in the morning. She said, "He'll be real mad!" But I guess she was desperate. She told me later that she burned them in a frying pan. He said, "What's that awful smell? This place has started smelling!" His wife replied, as she fanned the smoke about the room, "I'm trying to get the smell out." He started to get sleepy. She put the pan down and lay down herself. Finally, he woke up and said, "We'd better go to bed. It's getting dark!" She said, "No, the sun is just coming up. We slept all night!"

Meanwhile, I talked more kids into going back with us to school at the end of summer. Some quit after a year or two, but many stuck with it. There were twenty-one Seminoles in school at Cherokee when I finished high school in 1945. Back at home, Mrs. Abbey was hard at work talking with the school board, trying to open doors for Seminole children at the nearby Dania school. She was successful, and Seminole children were accepted there by 1947.

I couldn't believe I was getting near to graduating. I told my grand-mother the summer before I graduated: "This is my last year of school. I am graduating!" She smiled and said: "I'm glad you stayed with it and are finishing, even though I don't believe in school. It makes me happy to see you stay with whatever you believe in, because if you had quit before finishing, you would have been a failure. Learn your studies and finish them—like Indian doctors do." I had learned from my grandmother to set a goal and go after it. So I set my goals at an early age. To finish school was one goal. To work among my people and get them on their feet through health care and education were my goals for the future.

I wrote to Mrs. Stranahan shortly before graduation: "I hope that it will be possible for more to follow and as I saw children following in my footsteps toward an education I knew then that I would never quit school which my grandmother wished me very much to do, because it means ev-erything to me to see my tribe take an interest toward the school which we need so badly. All the years I have been in school I pray that someday all my people may realize the needs of an education and that my influence may mean something to them." I also reflected: "It was very hard for me to go against the old customs of the older people of my tribe; many, many times have our first three students been scolded and ignored for having anything to do with the white man's education, and the Christian religion. Some-times I almost thought I could not go on" (Jumper n.d.b).

In sewing class we had learned how to make dresses, so I made my own graduation dress. On graduation night, as I was walking up to get my diploma in my white dress, I knew that it would always be one of the happiest moments of my life. My tears fell, as I had fulfilled one of my dreams and my mother was there to share it with me. She had come all the way from Florida on the bus.

13

Nursing

Since I finally understood English, I began to interpret for my people when I came home every summer. They knew that I was going to study medicine, and they began coming around my home asking me to talk to the doctor for them about their illnesses and other things; so my job was cut out for me even before I finished high school.

Upon graduation from Cherokee, my next step was to go on to nurses' training to learn how to treat sick people, a position that was needed so badly among the Florida Seminoles. I returned home that summer for two and a half months. Then I had to leave home again, to begin training at the Kiowa Teaching Hospital in Oklahoma. There only Indian girls were taught, and upon completion of their training, they would return home to their reservations or would work at other Indian hospitals.

There were about thirty girls who entered training at the same time I did. Agnes Parker, my cousin, also finished high school at the same time, and she too entered this program, which would train us to be health field workers.

The nurses' training was very different from high school. It was hard work, and some of the girls began to drop out. Some cried because of the workload, and some got sick to their stomachs or fainted in the classes that we attended. It was really a challenge to stand and watch as a doctor operated on people.

We worked six weeks in each department. I particularly remember when I worked in obstetrics. I was to assist a doctor one morning to bring a child into the world. The doctor was to pass the baby to me once it had been delivered. I had done this a few times before, but at that instant, a girl called my name and I turned to look her way. Out of the corner of my eye, I saw the baby falling down. I grabbed it as it was slipping through my arms. I caught the baby's feet against me and dropped to the floor on my knees. There I was on the floor with my heart pounding, clutching the baby and thinking, "If I had missed the baby, it would have hit the floor and it would have been my fault." The doctor turned to look at me on my knees with the baby in my arms. He quietly said to me, "Next time we will pay attention. Won't we, Miss Tiger?"

Then I thought of how many points would be held against me, as this was definitely a bad thing that I had done. Maybe I'd even be sent home. It was a strict school, and we were supposed to know what we were doing. "No mistakes," the staff told us. "A mistake can mean a life!" I was sick over what I had done, but at class the next morning, I didn't hear anything. I expected at any moment to hear our chief nurse say, "Miss Tiger, would you please come to my office."

During everything I did, I either hummed or sang in the hallways. I had been called down on that. It was there at the school of nursing that I learned to work with a smile—regardless of what kind of mood I was in. Our chief nurse told us: "When you go out into the world to work, remember this: When you leave home, leave your troubles at home. When you enter your place of work, take up work troubles and leave all of your private problems at home. Never talk about your problems with your patients or the people with whom you work. When you leave work at the end of the day, leave your work there, and do not take it home!" I would follow this advice throughout my life wherever I worked. I never talked to anyone at work about my personal problems and never brought anything home from work.

Some people said, "You must have had a very happy life to smile all of the time." If they only knew half of the difficulties I had to endure! Only through my Savior was I able to deal with my life and make it to the next day and smile at people as I entered through the door. I learned that it doesn't hurt to have a pleasant face around people, even when you're crying inside.

Back home I was persecuted. Seminoles would chastise me, "You're not supposed to go to school." At Brighton and Big Cypress they would say, "She's a white woman. That's why she's doing it." They even told my grandpa that they would make medicine against me, but he told them, "Since she's Christian, she won't be harmed," and I believed it (Jumper 1998b). Yet in 1945 I wrote Mrs. Abbey, "I know I am going to face hardships and many hurt feelings because of many people but I'm not afraid for I know God will be with me through thick and thin" (Jumper 1945a).

Before I knew it, I had completed almost a year of nurse's aide training, and I was transferred to Shawnee, Oklahoma, to complete three months of field training with a public health nurse. I worked with Sac and Fox and Kickapoo patients. I learned to treat for worms there. There were few cases of worms in Oklahoma compared to the virtual epidemic in Florida, but that's where I learned to deal with them.

When I returned to Florida with my certificate for nursing and field training in 1945, I went to work at Jackson Memorial Hospital for one year, interpreting for the Indian patients and their doctors and nurses. [At this time no public health nurse was working with the Florida Seminoles, so the government placed Betty at the hospital until funds could be appropriated for a nurse assigned to the Seminole Agency (U.S. Department of the Interior 1946).]

Every time an Indian was admitted to the hospital, I was called off floor duty to help and interpret. I worked there until government money was placed into a program for me to work on the three Seminole reservations and among the nonreservation Indians along the Tamiami Trail. I had a route for about six months before the public health nurse, Esther Drury, arrived. She was a tall, skinny, redhead and a good nurse. She was from "out West," where she had been cured of TB, but she was scared to death of Seminole Indians!

We were stationed at the Dania (now Hollywood) Reservation in a little wooden building that served as our clinic. It had a living room (that we turned into a waiting room), a bedroom, a kitchen with an icebox for our medicines, and a bathroom. There were between seventy and eighty people living on the Dania Reservation by this time.

We traveled every two weeks to the other reservations—Big Cypress and Brighton—in the government's old 1941 Chevrolet sedan. We spent a good deal of time fixing flat tires on isolated roads in the hot sun. Other times, it rained, and we were bogged down in muck on inundated roads. There, we sometimes remained stuck until someone came along and pulled us out. The big yellow government truck picked us up from the main road to take us to Big Cypress, which was sometimes flooded. There were no direct roads to the outlying reservations like there are today. With good conditions and good luck with the car, it took us three or four days round trip. Sometimes we would stop under trees to have our lunch, and we would talk about what we were doing, saying, "We must be crazy to do this! In the hospital it was easy work, and we could be working there." Then we would laugh and get up and start off again.

I had returned to a struggle. My tribe was still against the new world. It was a tough road trying to convince the people that the medicine man could cure certain illnesses but wasn't familiar with white man's illness, and so that is why we needed the white doctors.

I'll never forget our very first trip to the Tamiami Trail. We stopped at the very first Indian village. The people were friendly to us and let us treat the kids and older people who had colds. We gave the kids bubble gum. For some it was the first they had ever had. As we continued west to the other villages, we would stop outside and ask if they needed our help, and I would explain that we would be by every two weeks.

When we got to the fourth village, we heard that there was an old lady very sick in this camp. The actual village was across a bridge that spanned the Tamiami Canal. We were almost over the bridge when a man came out of a chickee with a gun in his hand. "Stop!" he warned us. We stopped dead where we were. I said, "We are only here to see if you need our help and to let you know that we will be around every two weeks if you should need us."

"No help! We don't need you. We got Indian medicine man here. Get out and don't come back!"

I told him that we would leave, but he kept on, "I wish you all don't come on Trail!" We left without answering him.

Miss Drury said to me, "Very close." I was scared too, having a gun waved at us like that. My heart was beating a mile a minute, and I thought I was going to faint. "How did you feel?" she asked.

By then I was getting madder and madder. "I am disgusted with him! I happen to know that his brother is married to a white woman in town and has a child. His own family is living in a nontraditional way!"

We drove along the Trail, which paralleled the canal, and saw some kids in canoes gigging garfish, while others who were swimming closer waved at us. Farther on, a lady was standing in front of a big village holding a baby in her arms and watching things in the canal. We stopped, and I asked her what she was looking at. She told us that she was throwing bread in the water so her baby could see the fish that were feeding on it. We stood there watching the fish chasing each other and feeding on the bread.

Being scared from the recent episode, I jumped when Miss Drury nudged me on the arm and said, "Look, there is a man staring at us!"

He stepped forward and came to where we were all standing. Everyone had known me all my life, knew that I was the half-breed from the reservation. "What's with you?" he asked in Mikasuki.

"Nothing," I replied, "only that we have medicine that we are giving out if you all need our help."

"No. No want it," he replied to me in broken English.

I said, "Okay, but if you ever need us, we come by every two weeks, unless there are a lot of sick people. Then we'll come every week."

He looked at me as if to say, "Why are you telling me this? We have our own Indian doctors!"

Without a word I turned to go. I looked for my partner, but she was already in the car and had the engine running for a quick getaway! I laughed at her and said, "Where you going?"

"Miles from here!" was her reply.

"I thought you were here to work with the Indians?"

"No sir! Not when guns are pointing at me!"

"But he didn't have one," I reminded her.

She answered, "His eyes told me that somewhere nearby he had one!" We both laughed and went on.

Our usual routine began early every other Monday morning by going south to the Tamiami Trail. By late evening, we would arrive at Big Cypress and spend all day Tuesday there, leaving in the evening if we weren't needed there any longer. On Wednesday we'd be at Brighton Reservation. Sometimes, we'd stay until Friday morning, then head back to Dania.

We would have all week to get the medicines that we would need to treat the cases that we saw in the field. We used powdered penicillin. We had to mix it in sterile water until it was dissolved. We used a lot of isopropyl alcohol and Mercurochrome for cleaning wounds. We would leave these medicines with patients and tell them, "Tomorrow get white cloth. Clean your cut. Then pour some medicine on it again."

In those days, the primary medical problem, and the primary cause of child mortality, was hookworms. We would see the children's little bellies sticking way out, and they looked yellow from lack of red blood cells. They were going barefoot in dirty places, and they would get infected with the internal parasites through cuts on their feet. Many of them also had head *lice, which contributed to their anemia. Others had untreated sores on their bodies.*

Then there were seasons of bad colds and flu. We had to fight with chicken pox and measles until we started giving the people shots to prevent these diseases. When there was an epidemic, we would go on our rounds every week.

On the Trail, we would only stop at camps where the people welcomed us and let us treat them. Another medicine man had accosted me for aiding his patients and asked, "Are you 'selling them' to people who are taking them out West?" We decided to be selective about where we stopped after another medicine man accosted us. We would slow down as we neared a camp and look to see if someone would wave for us to pull over and help them.

One time we stopped to dress a cut that we had treated on our last trip. A young man about my own age came out and watched us doing that. After we had finished, he asked, "Why do you do all of this?"

"Because it's our job," I answered. "We are nurses. Why?"

He said, "I see you all passing by often, and many people are not nice to you, but still you come back. It's more than I could do."

I replied, "If you were hunting out in the Everglades and someone got hurt, would you walk away?"

"I guess not."

"Well, that's the same with us. We can't let sick people get worse and die just because some people aren't so nice. We can't walk away because we care for these people."

He shook his head and walked away.

There were other children who had been born into the same unfortunate circumstances as I. The discrimination of the traditional elders was still strong against half-breeds. The one or two half-breeds that were born each year were given away to Hollywood Reservation people, who wouldn't kill them. One child had been born of an illicit clan union, a blatant case of incest in traditional terms. I don't know why the child wasn't killed at birth. The mother would on occasion try to kill this child. I saved him once when she had thrown him in a canal to drown. He was only five years old. The child's paternal grandfather, a Christian Seminole man, took him to raise (Jumper 1998b).

I also was around when James E. Billie (the dynamic tribal chairman) was born. His father was white. Traditional people from the Trail came to the church grounds where we were. James was about four or five months old. They said that James's mother, Agnes Billie (Bird), should "get rid of him!" Agnes and I told the medicine men that if they threatened the baby again, we would turn them in to the agent (Jumper 1998b).

Time rolled on, and Miss Drury and I were still on the roads week after week. Most of our patients were superstitious and practiced Indian medicine and even witchcraft. I was never scared of traditional Indians, but I had been taught to respect them.

When someone died in the camp where they lived, even a camp on the reservation, it became off limits. No one would come out of the camp for four days, and you knew to stay away. On the Tamiami Trail where the villages had palmetto fences around them, they literally closed up. The relatives of the deceased, all of the close kin, stayed there and used medicine for four days. On the fourth morning, everything in the camp was cleaned, the yard was raked, all of the cooking dishes and utensils were washed, all cooked food was thrown out. All of the things belonging to the person who died were bundled up to be discarded. (It is believed that throwing away all of the belongings of the deceased makes it easier to forget that person.) Every evening, leaves of a medicine plant were burned to make the spirit of the dead person stay away.

The same leaves are also burned to calm people down a little. They are used on many sick people. (I gave these leaves to Mrs. Marmon to help her husband get some sleep.) My partner, Miss Drury, couldn't believe all these things. I just told her, "Live and learn," and we laughed.

I'm sure that we both thought about our encounter with the man and the gun every time we drove by his village on the Trail. One early morning about a year later, we were under way. I recall that there was a cool winter breeze and that from time to time a car with Indian men in it would pass on their way to buy food. As we approached the man's village, there was a figure in the road waving at us! I saw the little blue truck that I knew belonged to that man and said, "Uh oh."

"Betty, what are we going to do?" asked Miss Drury. "Shall I stop and turn around? Maybe he is trying to stop us from going in."

I was kind of nervous too. We were about twenty miles along the Trail. I was also a little mad at thinking he was meeting us way out here to try and turn us back! My thoughts were going round and round as I considered what I would say to him, but I wasn't going to let him try to scare us. As we neared, he was still in the road waving. I told Miss Drury to pull over to the side of the road, but she was so scared that she killed the engine in the middle of the Tamiami Trail!

I yelled to him in English in the gruffest voice I could muster, "What do you want?"

"Come help me!" was his surprising reply.

I jumped out of the car and ran to where he was.

"My wife," he said in Indian, "she's having a baby, and I'm having a flat tire. She's bleeding too much."

"Okay," I said. "Tell the nurse to turn the car around and don't scare her either! Talk to her in English!"

Somehow Miss Drury got her wits about her, turned the car around beside the truck, and helped us get the lady in the car. Away we went flying toward Miami and the hospital. I was in back with the patient, who kept crying and saying that she was short of breath. She was indeed losing too much blood. At last, we arrived at the hospital. We waited until we saw that she would be all right, then started back again out to the Trail.

We started laughing about how scared we had been. Miss Drury said, "I thought we'd had it! I wonder how he will treat us when we see him again."

Two weeks later, we found out. As we approached the camp, there were kids fishing in the canal. Miss Drury was uneasy, but I told her that we would stop. The man was there, messing with a fishing pole. He turned and looked at us. I yelled from the car, "How is the baby and mother?"

"Fine. Fine," he replied.

*We were about to take off, but he stopped us, saying, "Come see baby."
We went across the canal on the bridge, through the chickee store, and on to
the chickee where the mother was swinging the newborn baby in a hammock. This man, who had hated us, now couldn't do enough for us. He brought
cold drinks for us, then ran back with candy. "Stop when you go by," he told
us. After that, he was nice to us and never let us go by without a drink and
a visit.*

*For two and a half years we kept up this schedule. Then, in 1950, Dr.
Boettner, a doctor from Ft. Lauderdale, was hired by the government to
work with us at Dania Reservation. Dr. Rogers came later. They treated
many patients who were seriously ill. Sometimes we would have to run out
and bring sick people in from other reservations. If we went to Brighton or
Big Cypress, I would stop at Clewiston and let them rest, then on to Jackson
Memorial Hospital twenty miles south in Miami. By then, Broward General Hospital was also open in Ft. Lauderdale, which made things easier
for us. Other times, one of the patient's relatives who had a car would bring
the sick person in to us. But there were many sick people who never saw a
doctor. Some of them waited too long to get medical care and died before
they could be treated. We still lost many babies and children to hookworms.*

*The women were won over first. They were concerned about their chil-
dren. The husbands were against white doctors, but the women let me and
Miss Drury help. Many patients had never been treated by a white doctor
before. I would ask them to point to where they hurt, and the doctor would
then begin asking them questions while I interpreted. Many patients had
never been in a hospital either. Hospitals were a real nightmare for the
Seminole patients, and sometimes I had to do a lot of talking just to get
them in the front door. Special Commissioner Reverend Glenn wrote about
Seminole patients, "A hospital room may be crowded with the ghosts of
those who have died in it—ghosts who all through the night reach their
long and white arms down from the ceiling toward the suffering Indian"*
(U.S. Department of Interior 1933:7). *Special traditional medicine*

would have to have been made for hospital patients just because they had been in a place where people had died.

I even found that doing my job sometimes brought people to Christ. Bill Osceola's granddad was a mean, really tough medicine man and bundle carrier. He had cancer, and someone brought him in to Jackson Memorial Hospital. They operated on him, but the cancer had spread. Bill (one of the first Seminole ministers) tried and tried to reach him, but he never could. One day, the people at the hospital told me to talk to the old man.

He was so angry. I talked with him. I prayed for him because his illness was terminal. I kept talking to him. I tried to phone Bill, but he was not home, so I got a preacher from the hospital to tell him who God was. He was scared at first. The preacher started to read the Bible, and I translated. "How do I go to heaven?" he asked. "I'm ready." He accepted the Lord.

The next night his sister and his grandson arrived at the hospital. That old man began talking about God. He had changed from an angry, hateful person to a smiling happy man. He died two hours later, but he had been saved.

We also tried to tell the people about the spread of disease. We told them, "When flies go around, they are carrying sickness on their feet." They had always covered their food with canvas, but they started putting lids on food. Around 1948, in a Seminole report of the Florida Federation of Women's Clubs in which field nurse Esther Drury was mentioned, it was noted under "Sanitation" that "members of one camp who had never practiced covering their food, became converted when presented with certain evidence under a microscope" (Florida Federation of Women's Clubs 1948).

About the fourth year I worked as a field nurse, the government money ran out, so I began working without pay, still continuing to interpret and work with Dr. Boettner, who was still being paid. Miss Drury left for another position. Some patients who knew that I wasn't getting paid helped me with gas, and some gave me a few dollars here and there. Gas was only about thirty cents a gallon, so when I had two to three dollars' worth, I could make it. More often, I might get a hamburger or a chicken from a patient.

Sometimes I'd spend all night with a patient in the hospital. Whenever I was asked to go, I went. Sometimes I was asked to go to court when people were in other kinds of trouble. For seventeen years, from 1947 to 1964, I served my people in this way. They had a special name for me. They called me Doctor Lady.

14

War and Marriage

It was 1942. My brother, Howard, was seventeen, and he was almost ready to graduate from Cherokee. He was a real athlete, playing football, baseball, and basketball, and he also did some boxing. When he came home to Hollywood, he got a job at the Opa Locka Naval Air Station. But then Pearl Harbor was bombed on December 7. He enlisted in the marines on August 18, 1943, his eighteenth birthday.

Private First Class Howard Tiger was the first Florida Seminole, and one of only three, to enlist in that war. Our grandmother was not happy about his decision. She said, "No Indian should join the white people's services," and the older Indians all agreed. The medicine men were real mad. They said, "We knew this would happen if we let half-breeds remain in the tribe" (Jumper 1998c).

A newspaper reporter who interviewed Howard about his decision was puzzled for the same reason. Why would this young Seminole man join the service of a nation with which his people were still technically at war? My brother replied, "Let me shoot Japs and I'll be happy" (Ft. Lauderdale Daily News 1945). Well, he got his wish and was stationed in the Pacific.

In 1944 the trustees of the Seminole cattle enterprise voted to spend $28,000 on war bonds. This was an unusual action for a poor tribe. Their cattle had been quarantined for six years during an outbreak of deer-tick fever. Finally, in 1944 the quarantine was lifted, and they could sell the cattle (U.S. Indian Service 1944:1).

When I came home from Cherokee school, I worked in the laundry in Miami with George Storm and Charlotte Tommie. Every week I put aside some money to buy war bonds.

Meanwhile, entrenched on Iwo Jima with the Third Marine Division, Howard wrote his mother in the summer of 1945: "Guess you've heard about the Marines landing here. I'm right in the thick of things . . . It's really been Hell and I can't say much for the island." And in a letter to Betty, he reported, "We've cleared almost all of the Japs off the island" (*Ft. Lauderdale Daily News* 1945).

Then Mother got a telegram saying that Howard was missing in action. For two weeks my mother and I were at the Red Cross station in Ft. Lauderdale and waited for news about Howard. Then we got word that the Howard Tiger that was missing was from the Oklahoma Seminoles. My brother was found alive in a hospital. He had been blinded by shrapnel at Iwo Jima and had malaria. He was in the hospital for two months, but he was alive!

After returning home, Howard told us on his return that he had been on Iwo Jima when the U.S. flag was raised over Mount Suribachi. His son Mike recalled his dad telling him that "he was so tired when he got to the top of Mount Suribachi, that he just collapsed. He was right there when the other Marines were putting up the flag. The first one had fallen, and his buddies were putting up a second flag. He didn't have the energy to get up and help" (McDonald 1998a).

Moses Jumper (Panther) was the second Florida Seminole to enlist. He was born on the Dania Reservation in a chickee that today would have been right on the northeast corner of Stirling Road and Highway 441. He was my classmate at Cherokee, and we had always been friends. Moses joined the navy and also went to the Pacific Theater of War. I wrote Mrs. Abbey in 1945 that Moses had joined. "I hate to see him go because Indians at home [are] making such a fuss about it" (Jumper 1945a).

Moses was a gunner's mate on the USS Lexington when it was sunk by Japanese dive-bombers in the Coral Sea. It was such a horrendous experience—men were on fire, and Moses couldn't save them—that it caused him a lifetime of nightmares in which he replayed the scene of trying to pull his buddies out of the burning debris. He was also placed in the tenuous position of a coast watcher, infiltrating into the Pacific Island communities (Lamme 1948; Starts 1986).

I married Moses in 1946, after the war. That was the year when I began to make crafts to sell to tourists. First I went to Mr. Kester's "Pippin" Landing, then Al Starts's "Jungle Queen" Landing. Al Starts had the Jungle Queen tourist attraction on New River, where his sightseeing boat would stop full of tourists. Mother had worked at this attraction while I was in school. Selling crafts there made it possible for her to send a few dollars to us kids. The tourists would buy crafts and look at parrots and wild animals in cages. The income from crafts helped me out a lot (see West 1998b).

But what the tourists wanted most was to see an alligator wrestling show. The wrestler gets an alligator. He climbs on its back, opens its jaws, and shows the people how many teeth it has. Then he closes its mouth and puts it under his chin. This frees his hands so he can tie its mouth up. Flip it over onto its back, and the alligator's small brain makes it pass out. Then the wrestler calls it and touches its chin, and it flops over, awake.

Captain Starts asked Moses to be his star alligator wrestler. A wrestler could make $100 a day in tips if the tourists were generous. But by this time, Moses had already begun to drink to escape his memories of the war. When he was sober, he was a nice person and really smart. When he talked, he knew what he was talking about. At first, he'd just get drunk every three months or so, but later, alcohol consumed him. Sometimes, when he was too drunk to wrestle, I would get into the alligator pit myself. I did that because I needed to earn money to feed the kids. I wore my regular clothes, *my Seminole skirt and blouse. The women tourists got really excited.*

"Look! She's going to wrestle it!"

"That's right!" replied Captain Starts.

So from the start of our marriage, I lived with an alcoholic. Our first child, Rebecca Ann, was born in December 1947. She was the first Seminole baby born in Broward General Hospital. Rebecca Ann was afflicted with water on the brain [hydrocephalus]. *She couldn't move. We could sit her up, she could smile and laugh, but she was retarded. I was told to put her in a home, but I didn't. The doctors thought she'd die in four years or so. She required constant care.*

My mother took care of Rebecca Ann during the day when I was working. I quit going on the old route, as I now worked in the clinic with Dr. Boettner. We made a short run to the trail one day a week. Meanwhile, our son, Moses, Jr., was born in 1950. I also raised Boettner (named for Dr. Boettner) and Scarlett Marie. I took them in to raise because their parents couldn't raise them.

Our longtime missionary, Willie King, became ill in 1943 and moved back to Okeechobee. That left his Seminole congregation of twenty-two years without a minister. In 1945 he had begged me to take him home to Oklahoma and put him in the hospital when I left to go back to school at the Kiowa Teaching Hospital. He was later well enough to return to Okeechobee, where he had a home.

Meanwhile, back at Hollywood, Willie Jumper and Grandpa, the church's deacons, had to take over. Neither could read, but they could recite passages and knew some of the Bible stories. Most important, both of them could pray, and they carried on. They led the Wednesday night prayer meetings and the Sunday services. They told us the story of Jesus and had us sing songs that Willie King had taught us. My aunt Missy and my mother also helped in the church.

About a year later, Willie Jumper was getting sick. The two men talked again. Willie told Jimmie "you must go back to Oklahoma and see if some minister can come and take over the church and teach, I won't be here long."

So . . . Jimmie Gopher left for Oklahoma. He talked in church, after church, and asked if they had anyone who could come down to Florida and take over. For three weeks he visited churches, but finally came back to Hollywood without finding anyone.

When he got back, he saw that Willie was getting worse and could hardly walk to church anymore. Willie lived in a camp where the [Okalee] *Indian Village is today, and he used to walk carrying* [kerosene] *hand lamps. Sometimes he would fall. . . . Once some people had to help him up, but he still wouldn't quit. He made them take him to church. Near the end, my Mother would drive her Model T over to his camp and drive him to and from church.*

No one knew what would happen because those two men had kept the church going for nearly seven years. We were worried, but, God had plans.

Two weeks after Jimmie passed away, a man came walking up to our house and told my Mother he was looking for Jimmie Gopher. She looked at him and told him "he is gone. Gone home two weeks ago."

That man was Stanley Smith, a Creek pastor from Oklahoma. He had heard about the need for a minister when Jimmie was in Oklahoma on his second trip. Rev. Smith had traveled to Florida to talk to Jimmie about becoming a minister.

My Mother took Rev. Smith to the Old Cemetery on the Hollywood Reservation where both Willie and Jimmie were buried. Rev. Smith got down on his knees and prayed over their graves. We all stood around with tears in our eyes (Jumper 1998b).

15

Termination: A Wake-up Call

Around 1946, when Betty was interviewed by Mrs. Stranahan, she stated, "I want to help my people understand [what they need for their future] and to assist and encourage our young people to get an education and to become good citizens of Florida" (Jumper n.d.a). But despite Betty's encouragement, by 1953 only four Seminole students had graduated from high school (Committee of Seminole Indians 1953). They were Howard Tiger, Moses Jumper, Agnes Parker, and Betty herself. World War II, the general difficulties of being away from home, and the rigors of obtaining an education all contributed to this disappointing result. In 1953 the boarding school portion of Cherokee was closed. However, Mrs. Erma Abbey, head of Friends of the Seminoles, had already managed through her persistence and determination to have Seminole children admitted into Broward County schools in 1947.

As the foremost educated Florida Seminole, and the assistant in public health work, Betty was called on to give speeches touting the tribe's progress. She wrote this speech in 1947 (Jumper 1947).

The progress of the Seminole Indian in the past ten years is astonishing to those who know them best. We have surrendered our prejudice to education in the broader term, as measured thro[ugh] books, writing and visual methods; to Christian religion, we have turned for a brighter hope for our Spiritual life. We are working for better homes and a better way of life for the children. . . .

We, as the younger members of our group have made Great sacrifice[s] and suffered much rebuke at the hands of Our leaders and older members of our tribe, but we have Been true to the tradition of the Red Man's bravery in persecution and suffering.

Our persistence though faltering at times has won for us; with the assistance of trusting friends from the Government Agency, Woman's Clubs, Churches, Daughters of the American Revolution and many many other organizations all we thank so much. Our own Indian people from Oklahoma have been very good to us; to leave their own comfortable homes to come to encourage our feeble efforts to know the right way to follow to the new life. It has all been very hard, we know. We want to take our place in untangling the mistakes that have been made in this our country toward us because we are misunderstood and to many a mystery. We want the young people of the State of Florida and the United States to learn that we want to take our place in the community life and some of the responsibilities of its government.

I am deeply grateful for the education I have received and I want sincerely to use it in the interest of my people. There is much to do and we want your help too.

In late 1949, Superintendent Kenneth Marmon encouraged meetings on the three reservations to appoint planning committees that would discuss "the proposed plan of developing a ten-year program for all of the Seminoles" (Marmon 1949). Betty called the meeting for the Dania Reservation and was elected acting secretary.

In 1953, there were 918 Seminoles on the tribal rolls. This figure included all of the Indians—those who lived on reservations (60 percent) and included the majority of Christian churchgoers as well as traditional believers, and the nonreservation-dwelling traditionals who followed the medicine bundle leaders (40 percent). Only one-fourth of the population could speak English. Between 70 to 80 percent could not read and write. There was no general tribal organization, owing to the differences between the reservation and nonreservation Seminoles. These differences had also created or exacerbated major political problems, which the government didn't understand and therefore didn't acknowledge.

The turmoil of these times can be illustrated by a major incident involving the children of widower Joe Billie. Following his wife's death, Billie broke with tradition and demanded the return of his motherless children from their maternal grandmother, who was their legal guardian in the traditional clan system. The grandmother, Lillian Stone Bowers, wanted to raise the children traditionally in the Everglades, while Billie wanted them to "live in the ways of Christians and have schooling." Lawyers were called in on both sides; the sheriff, the governor, and the federal government became involved. Warrants were issued for a medicine man, the aging grandmother, and her son, the children's uncle, who was an important person in the children's traditional upbringing.

Indian sovereignty, international law, and a Christian father's rights were issues that pitted the reservation Seminoles against the Trail Miccosukees. Betty was the interpreter in the dispute, traveling by airboat with Sheriff's Department officials and lawyers to the isolated camp about four or five miles north of the Tamiami Trail. In hearings, the grandmother was deemed incapable of caring for the children, and they were returned to their father to reside on the Hollywood Reservation (Milne 1956; Hogan n.d.a, n.d.b).

The year 1953 was an eventful one for the tribe. Marmon received word that the government wanted to terminate the Seminoles as a tribal group. He presented the facts to the Seminoles. The big picture was that the government saw termination of Indian tribes as a way to cut the Bureau of Indian Affairs's expenses following World War II.

Officials from the Seminole Area Office, Muscogee, Oklahoma, met with the Florida Seminoles at the old Seminole Agency building on the Hollywood Reservation. Most of the Indians from the Dania, Brighton, and Big Cypress Reservations were in attendance, along with a few of the nonreservation "Tamiami Trail group." Resolution 108 stated: "Whereas it is the policy of Congress, as rapidly as possible, to make the Indians within the territorial limits of the United States subject to the same laws and entitled to the same privileges and responsibilities as are applicable to other citizerns of the United States, to end their status as wards of the United States, and to grant them all of the rights and prerogatives pertaining to American citizenship." This resolution, as well as the rough draft of the proposed bill that would provide for termination and the federal supervision of the Florida Seminoles' property, had been previously discussed, and it had been decided that a committee representing the three reservations and the trail should be appointed by their respective groups. There were 400 people from the Seminole reservations and the Tamiami Trail at the meeting. Betty Mae Jumper was elected secretary of the Seminole Indian committee. She recalled: "I got lots of votes, far more than the other two men who ran against me. I was surprised." But Betty had no political aspirations at that time. She, along with the other women, was content to aid the political process by cooking for the men's daylong meetings.

She and Moses did a great deal of interpreting during these troubled times. They explained what termination meant, what effect it would have on the Seminole people, why the Seminoles needed to fight against it, and how to fight it (by organizing in a formal way). But the Jumpers also knew that many of the Seminoles did not want to become organized. As Betty recalled: "We went around convincing people. It was hard. Some of our people thought maybe they [the Miccosukees] were right, that we should stay traditional, but most of them thought they'd go along with the plans to organize as the Seminole Tribe of Florida."

At a meeting on October 9, 1953, Mr. C. O. Talley, assistant area director of the Muscogee office, and other visitors explained the resolution and the termination proceedings. Following the meeting, the Seminole contingent met for a discussion and decided to "request that no action be taken on the termination of Federal supervision over the property of the Seminole Indians for a period of twenty-five years." This request was based on the fact that the government programs had not been established among the Florida Seminoles until 1933. The tribal group had advanced greatly since that time but "need[ed] guidance for a longer period and . . . look[ed] to the Federal Government for continuance of their supervision," wrote committee secretary Betty Mae Jumper (Committee of Seminole Indians 1953:3).

Mike Osceola (Bird) originally belonged to the nonreservation trail group, but he had become acculturated in the Miami tourist attractions and had his own personal agenda. He felt that the tribal people could manage to survive if they were terminated. "He was raised among the white people and knew how they lived. He had gone to school." Betty's brother, Howard, felt as Mike Osceola did. "He said that he believed that the Seminole could manage if they were terminated because they would have to!" Betty recalled.

At a public event, Betty told the audience of the Seminoles' desire to have "nice homes like you all," rather than chickees. Noting that the Seminoles' lack of education was "the reason we are so far behind," she asked the audience to write their congressional representatives and ask that the Seminoles retain their tax-free status for another twenty-five years while "we educate ourselves to work and learn to make more money" (Flagg 1954).

But the "organizationalists" far outnumbered the "terminationalists." Superintendent Marmon, who was himself a Pueblo Indian, discussed the organization process and how the Seminoles were not going to get help if they didn't try to help themselves. Still, they welcomed the aid of Mrs. Frank Stranahan, her Friends of the Seminoles, the Florida Federation of Women's Clubs' Indian Committee, and supporters around the state and nation who reiterated the Seminoles' plight in hearings before the federal representatives. Had it not been for these individuals and organizations that had worked with the Seminole parents and children for many years and who had faith in them, the tribe would probably have been terminated. As it turned out, the Seminoles' request for "twenty-five years" in which to become self-sufficient was granted (U.S. Congress 1954).

The initial task for the committee was to respond to the government concerning their possible termination. Betty wrote:

> Our Indians are still living in their native "chickees," open on all sides with a roof of cabbage palm leaves. Only two of the homes on Dania Reservation have running water, and only three or four have electric lights. There are no sanitary facilities on any of the reservations, with the exception of a few outhouses. During the coming years we must work to improve living conditions and attempt to create a desire for better homes and improvements of sanitation. Council houses on the three reservations are needed, so that frequent meetings can be held where we can meet in groups and plan to improve conditions, and study the problems of welfare, health, education and business management as problems applying to our people. (Committee of Seminole Indians 1953:3)

Some things had in fact gotten much better by 1953. Almost every Seminole family had a car, which meant that they had a better chance of getting to a hospital when they were sick or injured. There was a public health nurse, who worked with the people, and four area hospitals, which would accept Seminoles at the government's expense. The 1953 annual report of the U.S. Department of the Interior stated that "more Seminoles have taken advantage of our health services and for this reason, infant mortality has definitely decreased." (This was wonderful news to Betty.) In addition, there were other civic groups in the cities who were eager to help the Seminoles. According to the same report, "Some civic clubs in this area are furnishing vitamins, eye examinations, glasses and dental services to school children."

But along with these improvements on the health scene, diabetes had made inroads into the tribe. The annual report noted, "The counties are now furnishing insulin for diabetic Indians as they do for non-Indians." Diabetes is a disease to which Native Americans are very susceptible. It is linked with a lack of exercise and poor diet and was therefore virtually unknown among the Florida Seminoles in the early years. But over time, they became more sedentary reservation dwellers who traveled by car and shopped at stores full of processed foods and snacks. In 1953 Agent Marmon estimated that nearly 80 percent of the Seminoles' food was purchased at stores (Beebe 1946). When the incidence of diabetes among the Seminoles increased, Betty, as a health-care worker, decided to devote all her energy to the medical problems of her people. "I relinquished my position as secretary of the Seminole Committee," she recalled. "It wasn't for me. I told the committee, 'Get Laura Mae,' my husband's sister, 'to take over.' It wasn't [for] me to stay in an office. My life was nursing and there was plenty to do."

The sociopolitical differences between the Christian reservation-dwelling Seminoles and the nonreservation Miccosukees became very apparent during the 1950s termination proceedings. It would have been relatively easy for the reservation Seminoles to draw up the necessary documents to become a recognized tribe and to begin to receive moneys held in trust, but the Miccosukees were now involved. The decision-making process became tedious, as the demands of the latter group had to be formulated first, then voted on in the traditional complete-consensus manner, which was very time-consuming.

The reservation Seminoles' progressive movement was supported by Frank Billie of Big Cypress, a truck driver and road builder who had been trained as a medicine man. Billie has been described as a "great thinker" and promoter of progress. According to Betty, he "thought it would be good to become an organized tribe" and believed that "if we can become organized they [the government] would help us more." Frank Billie was a son of the adamant leader of the antireservation, traditional Miccosukee movement, Ingraham Billie. Though illiterate, Frank Billie would be elected as the Seminole

Tribe's first president. In 1954 Mike Osceola (Bird) brashly discussed in a newsaper interview those intratribal factions that could split families apart, classifying them as "Die Hards," "Progressives," and "Reactionaries" (Bellamy 1954).

Meanwhile, in 1955, the Seminole tribal members on the Hollywood Reservation were told that the Florida Turnpike, a toll road that was being built down the middle of Florida (now the Ronald Reagan Turnpike), was going to cut the reservation in half. Betty recalled: "They wanted to go through the reservation. Finally after meeting with them, it seemed we had no choice but to let it go through—so it did. We didn't have anyone to stand up for ourselves who knew how to fight against things that would affect us like that. We didn't want it to go through, but it did" (Jumper 1998b).

So in these difficult times, the Seminoles had factions within and without, and outside pressures to deal with, as they made their plans to establish and structure the new Seminole Tribe of Florida and move toward formal tribal recognition.

16

Reservation Improvements

After the Seminoles were saved from termination, they tried to prove themselves worthy in the government's eyes. Community leaders and wage earners on the Hollywood reservation worked on the reservation's appearance and the families' acculturation. They became engaged in a movement to upgrade the reservation housing.

The Tigers had long lived in the best house on the reservation, the dairy house that had been torn down and rebuilt. But it needed improvements. In 1941, while at Cherokee, Betty had written Superintendent Marmon, asking him to "build a porch and rest room at my place" (Jumper 1941). But for other, less fortunate students, it was hard to return from Cherokee to open-sided chickees with no electricity, no running water, and no sanitary facilities. The communal bathroom facility was in a lean-to around a tree, with a brown water well some 100 feet away.

By the mid-1950s all of the children on the Hollywood Reservation were in local public schools. Naturally, they wanted an environment like their classmates had. "The Seminole children feel they should live in homes now that they are attending White schools" (Sheldon Pressbook n.d.a). Thus, it was often these students who encouraged their parents to seek housing, which came equipped with hot and cold running water, a bathroom, and a kitchen.

The Friends of the Seminoles had worked hard to get the children accepted at the local schools; now they wanted their students to have the basic advantages at home that society had to offer. The group's membership fliers read: "Would you like to live in a 'chickee'? No Floors, no Walls, no water, no Privacy, no Sanitation. Why do Seminole live like that? Because they have no money to build houses because Banks or FHA cannot loan money on Reservation land because they have no one to help them get started. The Friends of the Seminoles are now offering that help" (Friends of the Seminoles n.d.).

The Seminoles did not own the reservation. The federal government did. How were they supposed to get financing for a loan from a bank to build a house when they didn't own the land? A section of the banking law did not allow banks to loan money for the construction of private residences on government property.

Another problem was that there were no tribal funds with which to build housing, and not many of the residents had a sufficient income to afford to build a home. However, some men were working as parking lot attendants and truck drivers, others were alligator wrestlers at area tourist attractions, and almost all of the women produced crafts for the tourist market. The average income for these individuals was estimated at fifty-five dollars per week. They could afford housing, but they couldn't get a home loan (Paulson n.d.).

Fortunately, Mrs. Stranahan, Mrs. Abbey, and Mrs. Francis D. (Ann Palmer) Sheldon had a plan. The Friends of the Seminoles had incorporated in 1949 and were now aided in their fund-raising and financial endeavors by the Community Chest, the forerunner of the United Fund (today's United Way). Additional aid came to the Friends from the State Federation of Women's Clubs' Indian Committee and local churches. With this strong financial backing, the Friends came up with a novel solution to the housing dilemma (*Ft. Lauderdale Daily News* 1949).

They appealed to their membership and to the public through a successful newspaper campaign asking for funds and services. They suggested that an interested person could cosign for an $850 loan to a Seminole family or buy a $100 membership as a gift or a loan to be paid back in ten years. The Ft. Lauderdale National Bank (now Sun Trust) agreed to handle all arrangements for the loans and to act as the collection agent (Daly 1956b).

The Friends of the Seminoles board member Mrs. B. E. Lawton stated, "We are hoping to find local people who will be willing to back this project" (Sheldon Pressbook n.d.a). One individual from Ft. Lauderdale contributed $1,000 to the fund, while another contributed $3,000. The *Miami Herald* wrote: "Indians living on reservations and unable to borrow from banks to build their homes would borrow from the fund to build small, one room houses which later could be expanded" (*Miami Herald* n.d.b; Revelle n.d.).

Indeed, financing was needed. Betty's own home, which she and Moses shared with her mother, Ada Tiger, needed another bedroom. But it was not until 1954, when the funds were provided in an unexpected way, that the Jumpers had the money to build an addition. Ada was bitten by an escaped monkey at the Chimpanzee Farm tourist attraction on Federal Highway where she sold crafts. The bite later became infected. She brought a suit against the attraction. The settlement money covered medical expenses and building costs for the extra room.

The first home in the Friends' Seminole housing project was obtained by Henry John and Juanita Billie (Panther clan) and their three sons. Billie, a parking lot attendant, qualified for the first loan. Betty's cousin Mary Parker Bowers (Snake clan) and her husband Joe, an alligator wrestler at the *Jungle Queen* tourist attraction, received the next loan.

The demand from Seminole families who wanted houses was so great that the Friends' building fund began to run low. The organization appealed statewide for contributions of one dollar (Friends of the Seminoles n.d.; *Ft. Lauderdale Daily News* 1955a, 1955b).

In February 1956 a rodeo arena was constructed at Dania Reservation, enabling the tribe to do its own fund-raising. The first rodeo was held February 28 through March 1, 1956, with 500 spectators on the first day. Tribal members handled most of the arrangements, directed the parking of cars, collected tickets, and sold refreshments. Betty recalled collecting money at the gate (Vinciguerra n.d.; Sheldon Pressbook n.d.c).

The *Ft. Lauderdale Daily News* reported, "The Indians had brought here from Brighton wild horses that had never had riders on their backs, as well as steers and bulls" (n.d.b). The first rodeo grossed $1,378, with a net of $500 after bills were paid for feed and for shipment of livestock from Big Cypress and Brighton. Yet it was a great start. A newspaper report enthused, "It was their first attempt at a community effort to help themselves, and it was a success!" (Sheldon Pressbook n.d.b, n.d.c; *Ft. Lauderdale Daily News* n.d.a).

Consecutive events held at the rodeo ground would fund Seminole trips to Tallahassee, Cherokee (North Carolina), and Washington, D.C., to discuss the tribe's formation and would serve as a benefit for the United Fund, which had long backed Seminole welfare projects to obtain clothing, schooling, jobs, and housing, and to further improve the living conditions for all residents of the Dania Reservation.

The Friends were thrilled with the next offer they received. Free cottages! S. E. "Doc" Northway of Pompano Beach's Northway's Marine Villas donated three partly furnished, white frame houses as he upgraded his business property. These buildings were moved to the reservation. Betty believes that her new home was one of the Northway cottages and that Charlie Billie Boy also received one (Daly n.d.; Jumper 1999a).

The Friends set up a revolving fund from which a Seminole family could borrow money and pay on a house. By the late 1950s the project was well under way, and the organization reported, "All membership fees for Friends of the Seminoles this year will be allocated to a housing fund for the Florida Indians."

By this time there were seven houses with electricity on the reservation. But it was not a smooth transition to move from a chickee, where cooking was done over an open fire, to a house with an electric stove and other appliances. Florida Power and Light sent a representative to the reservation. A county homemaking agent organized tours of drapery shops. The agent brought a portable house plan with miniature furniture, so that the women could move the furniture around and see how it would look in different places, a project which appealed to the husbands as well (*Ft. Lauderdale News* n.d.c).

Because the average income for reservation families was around fifty-five dollars per week, some could not afford to furnish their new homes, especially since they had to make monthly mortgage payments of eighteen to twenty-five dollars. The chairman of Indian welfare for the Florida Federation of Women's Clubs appealed to area residents in newspaper headlines such as "Lady Don't Throw Out Furniture!" (Sheldon Pressbook n.d.a).

A contest was held to select the reservation women who had made the greatest improvement in housekeeping from July to October 1956. The Hollywood Home Improvement Committee members of the Home Demonstration Council served as the judges. They gave points on tidiness, orderliness, food sanitation, and yard appearance. The winners were Betty's cousin Mary Bowers, first place; Martha Osceola, second place; and Betty Mae Jumper, third place. The prizes were household appliances and furniture awarded by the Salvation Army (Daly 1956a; Hogan n.d.b). Mary and Martha had two of the more modern houses. Betty's was an old one, with old appliances such as a kerosene stove and kerosene heater.

On November 11, 1959, Seminole Estates, the first subdivision on the reservation, was formally dedicated. This major reservation project was the result of three years of hard effort on the part of the Friends, the Seminole families, and political leaders. It had begun with Bill Osceola's CBS (concrete block structure) home and all of the imported cottages. The *Ft. Lauderdale Daily News* reported: "Some of the homes in Seminole Estates, the new development just west of the Turnpike, are remodeled houses moved to the reservation. Others are new CBS dwellings with air conditioning, pastel refrigerators, and built in ovens and stoves" (1959, n.d.a).

Government representatives were extremely impressed with the progress of the Florida Seminoles. Indian commissioner Glenn Emmons told the audience of 750 people, "I tell other Indians in the United States to look to the Florida Seminoles as an example." He called the new homes "one of the most remarkable achievements in the annals of American Indian History. I'm impressed by your continued desire for self-improvement. You have accomplished more than I thought could possibly be done since we first met in 1954" (*Ft. Lauderdale Daily News* 1959, n.d.b).

17

The *Seminole Indian News*

In 1961 a United Press International photo appeared in a local newspaper with the caption "Seminole Scoop": "Seminole Indians have many irons in the fire these days. They run their own tourist attractions, cattle ranches, and businesses. Now they've entered the newspaper field with a publication called the *Seminole Indian News*" (United Press International 1961). The *Seminole Indian News*, a monthly publication, was the creation of coeditors Betty Mae Jumper and Alice Osceola.

At that time, Betty Mae Jumper was employed by the Broward County Board of Public Instruction as a visiting teacher on the Dania Reservation. She had held that position for the past two years. She was also serving as a director on the board of the Seminole Tribe of Florida, Inc., which was responsible for the control of Seminole lands. Alice Osceola was a senior at Southwest High School in Miami. As the first Miccosukee to go through high school, she was also serving as secretary of the newly formed Miccosukee Seminole executive council.

Betty went to the Tamiami Trail and discussed with Alice the idea of a newspaper that would serve both the Seminoles on the reservations and the Miccosukees. She and Alice further discussed the project with Morton Silver, an acquaintance of Alice's who was the legal council for the Miccosukee tribal movement. Betty recalled: "He told [us] how to do it. He helped us put it together. Then he told us that the only way we could run the paper was to sell it. So we started selling it for ten cents per paper in Miami. My daughter, Scarlett Marie and Howard Tiger's daughter, Russella, sold the paper in front of a supermarket. The *News* cost [us] seventy-nine dollars an issue [to produce].

"We did all of the reporting, then took the material directly to Mr. Silver in Miami. He proofed it. He told us why it needed to be this way and that way, corrected it, and gave us encouragement."

Silver had played an important, though controversial, role in his support of the Miccosukee movement through the 1950s. But this newspaper, for which he served as an adviser, had the potential to be a boon to both the Seminoles and Miccosukees.

An editorial in the second issue, September 1961, stated under the tag line "A Free Seminole Press": "The coeditors of the Seminole Indian News, in response to hundreds of queries, want to repeat that this newspaper is owned and published and controlled by Seminole and Miccosukee individuals. This newspaper is free of all censorship by tribe, state or federal government. Its policy is to print the truth. It is a free newspaper in the best tradition of the American press" (Jumper and Osceola 1961b).

The editors were concerned about their viewpoints as they represented two culturally similar but idealistically diverse tribal entities. They admitted to their readership, "Lots of times the editors will not agree in their editorial viewpoints. So they will sign their editorials, so that readers will know whom to blame" (Jumper and Osceola 1961a).

The editors thanked their first advertisers, who included Metropolitan Dade County; The City of Miami; George Stacy, of Musa Isle Tourist Attraction; Tony Benedetto, president of the Hialeah City

Council; Virgil Harrington, U.S. Indian agent; Bill Osceola, of the Seminole Okalee Indian Village; and Mrs. Evelyn Harvey, president of the Co-Workers Woman's Club.

Letters of encouragement and congratulations came from Congressmen Billy Mathews and Sidney Herlong, Florida secretary of state, Tom Adams, Florida comptroller Ray Green, Florida attorney general Richard Erwin, Florida agricultural commissioner Doyle Conner, and Judge David Hefferman, among others. Letters printed in the second issue had been received from the newly appointed U.S. Indian commissioner, Phileo Nash; M. M. Tozier, of the U.S. Bureau of Indian Affairs; Senator George Smathers; Thomas D. Bailey, Florida's superintendent of education; Senator Spessard L. Holland; and Congressman Paul G. Rogers of Florida (Jumper and Osceola 1961b).

The *Seminole Indian News* was set to play a leading role in Seminole politics. An editorial in the inaugural issue (August 10, 1961) read: "The full Miccosukee and Seminole staff of this newspaper recommends and urges every Indian registered voter of the *Seminole Tribe of Florida* to vote for Betty Mae Jumper for the Tribal Council representative from the Dania Reservation. Over the many years, Betty Mae has demonstrated her public spirit, outstanding ability and integrity as a tribal leader. She has done as much, if not more than any other member of the Seminole Tribe of Florida to improve the welfare and living conditions of her people. She is well known as a fearless, tireless and dedicated worker for her people. Betty Mae Jumper is progressive and a registered democrat. She will be a valuable asset to the Tribal Council" (Jumper and Osceola 1961a).

Meanwhile, Betty's brother, Howard Tiger, one of the first councilmen of the Seminole Tribe, had been fired by the chairman of the Seminole tribal council, Reverend Billy Osceola, from his position as organizer and first recreation director on the Dania Reservation. The *Seminole Indian News* carried the story under the heading "Iwo Jima Veteran Fired" (Jumper and Osceola 1961a).

The *Seminole Indian News* backed other candidates and later reported: "The five candidates that the *Seminole News* staff supported for board of directors and councilmen of the Seminole Tribe of Florida won in the election on August 14." Then, in selecting the tribe's president, the board members gave four votes to Jimmy Cypress and four to Howard Tiger. To break the tie, a special election by all tribal members was called on the three Seminole reservations (Jumper and Osceola 1961b).

The editors promoted the election process. A sidebar in the first edition proclaimed: "Get out and vote in Aug. 14 election" (Jumper and Osceola 1961a). Prior to the election a *News* editorial told readers to "Vote For Howard Tiger!" because "Howard Tiger, a candidate for president of the board of directors of the Seminole Tribe of Florida, Inc. is the best educated candidate for the position, and very well qualified to manage the business affairs of the tribe. He will stick to his word and his promises. Howard is a veteran of the U.S. Marines in World War II, and fought at Iwo Jima. He is the father of four children. The *Seminole Indian News* is proud to endorse him as president" [signed "BJ"] (Jumper 1961a).

Meanwhile, in news from the Tamiami Trail, Miccosukee tribal leaders voiced their consternation over their first U.S. agent, Reginald C. Miller, who had been sent from the U.S. Department of the Interior. The Miccosukees made it clear that they wanted to be represented by lawyers of their own choosing. They discussed their concern over the inherent tribal differences between themselves and the Seminoles.

The fall of 1961 was a very busy time. The Seminole and Miccosukee Tribes were coming into their own politically. Governor Ferris Bryant spoke at the dedication of Krome Avenue, an important north-south artery connecting western Dade County with the Tamiami Trail and the closest road to the Miccosukee headquarters. At the event Governor Farris Bryant promised Mike Osceola, Seminole tribal councilman, and Betty Mae Jumper, Seminole tribal director, "that he would look into the possibility of constructing a connecting road between the Big Cypress and Andytown" (Jumper and

Osceola 1961b). This road would be Alligator Alley, recently incorporated into I-595.

Having a newspaper as a forum was a real novelty and a major break with tradition for the tribal peoples. Responses published in a column titled "What They Said . . ." showed their mixed feelings toward the news vehicle. Many mistrusted and feared it, especially the large numbers who were isolated and illiterate yet facing the new responsibility of voting in a nontraditional, democratic system. On the other hand, Charlie Billy Boy of the Dania Reservation said: "Go ahead and write the newspaper. Write everything that's true." Mike Osceola, of the tribal council in Dania, stated: "I don't see how anybody can stop this newspaper from printing the truth." A Seminole woman on the Brighton Reservation questioned officials who were discussing the newspaper at a meeting in Brighton: "What have you all been hiding that you think they will come out and print the truth?" But political leader Billy Osceola, a Baptist minister from Brighton, claimed the newspaper printed "Lies. Lies. Lies" and "should be stopped." Headed by the Reverend Osceola, the tribal council formally announced that it did not "condone or agree with the editorial policies of this newspaper." Readers were reminded by coeditor Alice Osceola that the newspaper was "a private enterprise" and "free of all censorship" (Osceola 1961). When questioned about Billy Osceola's attitude in light of their longtime working relationship, Betty replied that he "didn't understand the idea of the newspaper."

The newspaper also became a forum for both editors to publicly thank those who had provided such welcome aid to tribal members over the decades. Betty praised Mrs. Frank Stranahan: "She helped so many Indians to go to school. She gave many of us our first dresses. Her kind and intelligent help has made the lives of so many of us richer." Similarly, Alice Osceola praised Mrs. Evelyn Harvey for her aid to Miccosukee welfare (Jumper and Osceola 1961a).

Howard Tiger was elected president of the Seminole Tribe of Florida, Inc., on September 19, 1961, in a landslide election over his opponent, Jimmy Cypress of Big Cypress, and succeeding the former president, the Reverend Billy Osceola. The president was the highest position in the Seminole Tribe. It was a full-time, salaried position. Howard rode through Seminole Estates at midnight in a Model T, blowing his horn. He wrote to the *Seminole Indian News*: "Dear Friends, I wish to thank your newspaper for endorsing me as a candidate for President of the Board of Directors for the Seminole Tribe of Florida, Inc.

"Thanks to the people who elected me. I shall try to live up to your expectation.

"Best of luck with your newspaper and may it grow with each edition" (Tiger 1961).

But this was not to be. Betty became very ill. She was rushed to the hospital and diagnosed with an acute case of ureic poisoning, which almost took her life. She was hospitalized for seven weeks, and when she was finally discharged, her convalescence was slow. Young Alice Osceola could not carry on by herself, and the fourth issue of the *Seminole Indian News* was its last.

The Miccosukee Tribe of Indians of Florida would gain federal recognition in 1962.

18

Hail to the Chief

When we became organized, we took steps forward to fight in the white man's world at tables, instead of with bows and arrows and guns. We learned how to fight in such a manner that things began coming our way. We found out that we needed money, so we borrowed from the government. Also we learned that there were grants out there that we could obtain to hire our tribal people to do jobs on the reservations.

Betty Mae Jumper

As we have seen, Betty had been involved with the Seminole Tribe's organizational process since the initial termination threat in 1953. At that time, she was elected to serve as secretary of the Seminole committee. When the tribe formally organized in 1957, she was elected vice chairman of the tribal council, serving under Chairman Billy Osceola.

The tribe was set up with two governing bodies: the tribal council, under a chairman, which deals with the social and general welfare problems of the tribe, and the board of directors, under a president, which administers the tribe's business affairs. To link the two bodies, the chairman of the tribal council—often referred to as the chief of the Seminole Tribe—also serves as vice president of the board of directors, and the elected president of the board also functions as vice chairman of the tribal council.

Education continued to be an important issue for Betty. During the late 1950s she served as the tribe's unofficial truant officer. Playing hookey was not tolerated on her watch. Christopher Billie, who hid in the cow pasture on the Hollywood Reservation, recalled: "One minute I could see her driving a van down the road. The next minute she was driving right through the pasture, that van bumping up and down, her head banging off the roof, the cows running one way and us running the other. . . . Everywhere we turned, she was there. We finally gave up and she hauled us back to school. Gave us a shower and brought us into school. I still don't know how she did that" (Gallagher 1994:17). The present, fifth-term tribal chairman, James E. Billie, remembered his own run-in with Betty: One day, when he should have been in school, she found him at the reservation rock pit. His excuse for playing hookey was that he had no shoes. Betty took him downtown to the shoe store. The clerk was astonished and asked, "Well, where is the new pair you got last week?" "Where are they?" Betty demanded. James replied that those shoes had "fallen" into the rock pit! He got a spirited lecture and a new pair, and he was taken to school.

In 1956 Betty's son, Moses Jumper, Jr., turned five and was eager to attend school. But one month after he started at Dania Elementary with his friends from the reservation, the Jumper family was notified that Moses's birth date was four days after the cut-off date for the first-grade class. He was devastated. The Friends of the Seminoles came to Moses's aid by offering him a scholarship to Pine Crest, a prestigious private school in Ft. Lauderdale (which had the only campus pool in town!). When he graduated from kindergarten in 1957, Moses was among the top ten of fifty-one students. Pleased by his performance, the Friends decided that his annual $612 scholarship would be renewed "as long as he wants it" (Jones n.d.). Moses acquired the name Big Shot from his tribal peers for being the first Seminole to attend a private school (*Miami Herald* 1957).

The school was thirteen miles from the reservation. Betty drove fifty-two miles a day. One morning when her old truck was not running, she started off taking Moses to school by bicycle but was soon picked up by an acquaintance.

In 1959 Betty was elected to a four-year term on the board of directors under President Bill Osceola. Seminole families on the Dania Reservation continued to opt for a more modern lifestyle and were enthusiastically supported in their efforts by the Friends of the Seminoles. In December 1960, three families were ready to move into their own homes. Mrs. Frances Sheldon told the *Ft. Lauderdale Daily News*, "They would move in tomorrow, if they just had mattresses." The families were those of Minnie Doctor and her four children; Randolph Jimmie, his wife, and their three children; and Mr. and Mrs. Johnny Tucker and their five children" (*Ft. Lauderdale Daily News* 1960a).

Right below this article, which was titled "You Too Can Help the Indians," was one with the headline "Reservation Casino Spurned by Seminoles." This juxtaposition was ironic; it was obvious that the Seminoles desperately needed money, yet they turned down a venture that would generate lots of it. Betty did not recall the casino issue but commented that Bill Osceola "was a Christian and a preacher and didn't believe in gambling." The unidentified Miami gambling interests dreamed of "setting up a plush gambling casino on the [Dania] reservation." In a newspaper interview, Osceola stated that the Seminoles had a "legal business" in the Arts and Crafts Center and Indian Village on the corner of State Road 7 and Stirling Road, which had opened in 1960. The businessmen had "said this would be a good location." Indeed, it is near today's lucrative Bingo palace (*Ft. Lauderdale Daily News* 1960b). It would take another decade and a chairman of another mind-set before the Seminoles began to explore their sovereign rights, leading to the introduction of tax-free tobacco shops and then lucrative gaming ventures on the reservations. The result was unprecedented tribal prosperity.

A special act of Congress in 1961 had authorized the Seminoles to lease property on the Dania Reservation for a period of up to ninety-nine years. This proved to be an economic boon for the poor tribe, which could now earn income from businesses and industries on the 300 acres of reservation land that fronted on State Road 7 (Highway 441).

The progress report of the Seminole Tribe for 1962 noted that there were "sixteen new modern CBS homes built on the Dania Reservation, ten modern remodeled homes and eight modern rental homes." By this date the business section of the tribe—that is, the Seminole Tribe of Florida, Inc.—had its own revolving credit program for tribal families, which made loans to qualified individuals. The report concluded, " At the present time, all of the residents of the Dania Reservation live in modern homes" (Seminole Tribe of Florida 1962).

At the end of her 1959–63 term on the council, Betty recalled, "I quit nursing for free for the tribe and went to work off the reservation at Heritage nursing home near Holy Cross Hospital in north Ft. Lauderdale. This business handled the rehabilitation and convalescence of patients. I worked there until 1966. I needed the money for the kids to go to school with. I needed to get back into working in the medical field." But tribal members continued to make requests for her services on a regular basis. "People were still coming to me for medical help; to interpret when they were in jail, to go to court with them. I helped them still."

In 1966 Chairman Billy Osceola acquired some money from the government and asked Betty to quit her job in Ft. Lauderdale and come back to the reservation and help him. She was then able to get paid for taking sick people to the doctors—work she had been doing for so long on her own. On slow days, she helped out with the Head Start program.

Betty's brother, Howard, continued to be one of the most important people in her life. As discussed earlier, the siblings had endured years of discrimination when they were the only half-white children in the tribe. Betty had always stuck up for her little brother when necessary—one of the reasons that she learned to be such a fighter. She was very proud of him when he excelled at sports at school and when he went to fight in World War II. As an adult, Howard offered her strong support and encouragement to enter the political arena. "He was the one that suggested that I run for chairman," she recalled. "He said, 'You have a better chance. You can do it. I'll help you out, but you can do it.'"

Barbeques have long been the Seminole politicians' main vehicle for meeting their constituents and winning votes, but there were no barbeques when Betty ran for chairwoman in 1967. "Why we could barely afford bologna and cheese sandwiches, *sofki*, potato chips, *lapalee* (pan bread), and we drank coffee and Koolaid!" she said. Betty held "campaign meetings" on all the reservations. Being the first trilingual candidate for chairman gave her a great advantage not only as a speaker but also as an interpreter.

Just before Betty's election, there was a terrible tragedy. Howard died on the reservation as the result of a freak accident. Betty recalled the painful details: "He died after a tractor ran over him. A truck loading muck got stuck. Howard got on his tractor to pull it out. Then the chain broke, so he put the tractor gear in park position and began to repair the chain. Somehow the gear slipped into operation. He was crushed against the truck. He was tall, so he reached over to push the gear back into park position. He didn't know his leg was broken and he slipped and fell. Then, the tractor crushed him" (Kirk and Cunninghan 1981). Seeing Howard lying in the coffin, "I thought I couldn't take it. Maybe I'd pull out [of the election]," she said. "But I promised him I'd go ahead and I did it."

The grieving candidate had staunch supporters. At three o'clock in the morning of May 9, 1967, when all the votes were counted, Betty Mae Jumper became the first chairwoman (and the only one to date) of the Seminole Tribe of Florida. She was forty-four years old. With her election promise "to improve health, education, employment, welfare, law and order and housing conditions" on the reservations, she had beaten her opponent, Jack Micco (Bird clan), by a vote of 170 to 116. This was a real vote of confidence because Betty's Snake clan remained tiny, having never recovered from the Seminole wars and the additional casualties of the nineteenth century. She had won an election not only against a man but against one from a large clan! Her husband, Moses Jumper, Sr., was elated. "I knew she'd scalp him! I'm real proud of her. I feel like George Wallace of Alabama. She's my Lurleen," he told a *Miami News* reporter (Glass 1967). (At the time of Betty's election, Moses Jumper, Sr., who had wrestled alligators for seventeen years at the Jungle Queen attraction, was working with the tribe's cattle program at the Brighton Reservation.)

Betty officially took office on June 5. The position of chairman was not the prestigious position that it is today. While her supporters were lucky to have had bologna sandwiches during her campaign meetings, the incumbent for the board position was serving up spareribs to woo voters. This was because in those days only the president of the board of the Seminole Tribe of Florida, Inc., received a salary. The newly elected president would earn $8,300 per year. Chairwoman Betty Mae Tiger, the chief of the Seminole Tribe, received nothing. She had to hold down a job coordinating the tribal clinics on the three reservations in order to make ends meet. However, Betty was a woman with a mission for her tribal people, and their acceptance of education was at the forefront of her plan.

Betty made the news. On the front page of the *Miami Herald*'s "For and about Women" section, Beverly Wilson wrote: "Behind a modern desk surrounded by business-like file cabinets and "in" and "out" baskets, . . . Seminole Betty Mae Jumper is out to create a new image for Seminole women. The nation she helps govern has citizens whose concerns range from keeping the Great Spirit's secret deerskin medicine bundle with its burden of herbs, stones and dried animal parts, to preventing their teenagers from drag-racing on the streets" (Wilson 1967). Meanwhile, the well-meaning *Miami News*—in these decades before "political correctness"—boldly proclaimed, "Squaw Now 'Big Chief' of Seminole Braves" (Glass 1967).

Betty was the last chairman in the period from 1957 to 1971, which

Harry A. Kersey, Jr., author of an important trilogy on Seminole history, has termed the Seminoles' "lean years" (1996:79). Beginning with a treasury of just thirty-five dollars, Betty, as chairman of the council and vice chairman of the board, brought it up to half a million dollars by leasing reservation land along State Road 7 (Highway 441), planting groves of lemons on the Big Cypress Reservation, and borrowing from the government. Kersey has suggested that the political power play between the stronger board and the weaker council, which, among other things, denied a salary for the head of the tribal council, served to weaken Betty's effectiveness as chairwoman (1996:116). "I could have gone ahead, full speed ahead, if I had had money to travel, to get to Washington. But with no money, I could hardly do anything," Betty said.

But on a lighter note, President Joe Dan Osceola suggested to the chairwoman that they host a powwow to get tribal members together. Linda Tiger served as secretary. With clothing contests, contests of skill, games, and a mock Green Corn Dance, Seminole Fair was born. In later years, Plains Indian dancers, Aztec dancers, southwestern dancers, a professional rodeo, and native foods were added, and the event evolved into the Seminole Tribal Fair and Rodeo, which continues to this day.

The chairwoman broadened the tribe's political base and welfare prospects by taking a leading role in the organization of the United Southeastern Tribes (USET) (now the United and Southeastern Tribes). The formal ceremony that established the organization took place October 4, 1968, on the Qualla Boundary, Cherokee, North Carolina. USET was a political organization that would give the tribes in the Southeast more lobbying power in Washington. The founding tribal chairmen and chairwoman of USET belonged to the federally recognized Seminole Tribe of Florida, the Eastern Band of Cherokee Indians, the Mississippi Band of Choctaw Indians, and the Miccosukee Tribe of Indians of Florida. Because these tribes resided far from the Indian centers of population in the West, a situation created by removal, they had been neglected by the Indian Health

Service's area office, located in Oklahoma City near the greatest number of tribes. So the leaders of USET lobbied for—and won—improved health services for their tribes.

Their Declaration of Unity proclaimed the following objectives:

- To promote Indian leadership in order to move forward the ultimate desirable goal of complete Indian involvement and responsibility at all levels in Indian affairs.
- To lift the bitter yoke of poverty from our peoples through cooperative effort.
- To promote better understanding between Indians and other Americans.
- To negotiate for more effective use of existing local, state and Federal resources.
- To provide a forum for exchange of ideas.
- To combine our four voices so our one strong voice can be heard clearly.
- To dedicate ourselves to improvement of health.
- To obtain for ourselves and our descendants the highest level of education.
- To reaffirm the commitment of we four tribes to the treaties and agreements heretofore entered into with the Federal Government, the spirit of which was restated on March 6, 1968 by the President of the United States.

The declaration was signed by Betty Mae Jumper, chairwoman of the Seminole Tribe of Florida; Buffalo Tiger, chairman of the Miccosukee Tribe of Indians of Florida; Emmett York, chairman of the Choctaws, and Walter S. Jackson, principal chief of the Eastern Band of Cherokees.

The USET team met quarterly in various states. The first formal meeting was in Atlanta, Georgia, in July 1969 and included representatives sent by the governor. Betty recalled: "If we needed help from a certain state, we had a meeting there. We put Seminoles and Miccosukees together because we had the same governor. A. J. Ryan was our lawyer who attended these meetings." In November 1969 Florida hosted the meeting, held at the new Miccosukee School on the Tamiami Trail.

The fact that USET had become important as an Indian forum was witnessed by those federal agencies who felt compelled to attend the conference: the Department of the Interior's assistant secretary, a representative of the Office of Economic Opportunity, a director of the U.S. Public Health Service, and the director of the National Council on Indian Opportunity (*Orlando Sentinel* 1969).

But again, the southeastern tribes' participating chairmen and chairwoman faced the challenge of trying to locate the funds from their tribal coffers to travel to Washington and to meetings in their respective states. Betty, who sometimes had to borrow travel money, recalled driving around in Washington until she and her colleagues found an inexpensive motel. Sometimes they had a car, but usually they took the bus.

In April 1970 the commissioner of Indian affairs, Louis R. Bruce, paid a visit to the Florida Seminoles and met with Betty, tribal president Joe Dan Osceola, and a crowd of some 200 Seminoles. Betty was especially impressed with Bruce's emphasis on the development of youth.

The youth were very important to Betty, who remembered her own social isolation, her educational needs, frustrations, and aspirations. She noted in news articles: "The younger generation want modern things. We want them to have clinics, gymnasiums and schooling. But we want them to have respect for heritage, too" (Kelly 1970). "Some will come back to the tribe, others won't. I'm hoping some of them will grow up to take over the government programs which are being planned for the Indians. We need leaders and college graduates." She told a reporter, "Our kids [on the reservations] are doing the same things all American kids are—they like the music and the clothes. Very few have become hippies" (Griffith 1970).

The National Council on Indian Opportunity, established in 1968, was the first viable program to aid impoverished Indian tribes that sought solutions to housing, education, and land problems on their reservations. It was the brainchild of Richard M. Nixon. In 1968, as the Republican presidential candidate, he had campaigned with the Native Americans in his thoughts. The *New York Times* (1968) reported: "R. M. Nixon deplores plight of Indians and mistakes made in caring for them. Pledges efforts to improve their lot." During Nixon's presidency the Labor Department allocated $8.4 million in emergency employment aid funds for public service jobs for Indians (*New York Times* 1970a). The House approved a bill authorizing $300,000 a year to finance activities of Nixon's National Congress on Indian Affairs (*New York Times* 1970b).

The chairwoman of the Seminole Tribe of Florida was being noticed and singled out for the same determination that had landed her the highest tribal position. She received an appointment from President Nixon to serve on his newly organized National Council on Indian Opportunity. On August 31, 1970, she went to Washington, D.C., to be sworn in by the U.S. House of Representatives for a two-year term. It was a prestigious government committee appointment, and Betty's involvement in this national welfare project again provided excellent exposure for the Seminole Tribe of Florida, which stood to gain in the areas of education and health (*Ft. Lauderdale Daily News* 1970).

Betty recalled sitting around having a cup of coffee with Nixon. Vice President Spiro Agnew was designated to travel with the committee members on their trips to various reservations. She discussed President Nixon's efforts to improve Indian welfare: "He really went all out for it. He gave Blue Lake back to the [Taos Pueblo] Indians [in New Mexico]. He said, 'If you think you're doing right, go on in and do it and I think I'm doing right.' I was in Washington when he signed the bill to give [Blue Lake] back to the Indians. We went out to Blue Lake. We on the Indian Opportunity Council helped to push for that."

The committee's projects also took them to Nome, Alaska, where a tunnel was built for native children to travel from their school to the dining facility. While scholars are only now putting a more positive spin on Nixon's presidency, the Seminole Tribe of Florida has always held him in high esteem because of his efforts to right injustices to Native Americans. "He was good to us Indians" is Betty's succinct assessment.

Betty received her first major award in November 1970. At the National Seminar for American Women held in Denver, she was named one of the "Top Indian Women" of the year for earning national recognition and working tirelessly on behalf of fellow Native Americans,

During her four-year term as chairwoman of the Seminole Tribe of Florida, she initiated and managed some of the first federal grants received by the tribe. A local newspaper quoted her as saying: "The Indian wants to earn what he gets. He does not want handouts. Before, the Indian wrestled alligators, made beads and dolls for tourist attractions. But we try now to bring jobs on the reservation. Some of our people already help build trailers as jobs" (Kelly 1970).

In 1971, as her term as chairwoman drew to a close, Betty's plans were indefinite. She told a reporter: "The job's been a lot of work and I enjoy helping my people in any way I can, but I just haven't decided whether I'll try for another term. I'll wait and see" (Griffith 1970).

19

A Legend in Her Own Time

As it turned out, Betty Mae Jumper did decide to run for a second term. Her opponent, Howard Tommie (Bird clan), was approximately ten years younger than Betty, and this generation gap would cost her the election.

The Florida Seminoles had seen drastic political change. Conversions to Christianity had disrupted the traditional political hierachy, with the political power shifting from the elders to younger converts. The elders, who were strong in medicine and had traditionally been in unchallenged political control of the Seminole people, did not pursue formal tribal politics. And so, from the time of tribal formation in the 1950s to the 1970s, the elders were not elected, and the positions were held by Christians who often used their new religion as a political platform. They made use of their education and new ideas to take the reins of government.

The same factors had probably worked in Betty's favor in 1967, when she was a youngish forty-four-year-old. She was the first formally educated Seminole, trained in the medical arts, outspoken, trilingual, a Christian, and a conservative. By contrast, her opponent, the male incumbent, was an illiterate, lay minister. But in 1971 young Tommie's platform was far more aggressive than Betty's. Whereas her platform was concerned with education and infrastructure, and appealed to the religious and older people, Tommie stressed a new order of tribalism, endorsing bucking the establishment to promote tribal self-help and sovereignty issues.

He received votes from more savvy, younger tribal members, which, coupled with the support of the largest clan, won him the election. Chairman Tommie quipped to a reporter, "I do belong to a large clan, and that was very helpful" (Liss 1975).

Away from the political arena that spring, Betty pursued an annual activity out in the woods that she loved. For the past fifteen years, two weeks before Easter she had cut immature palmetto frond sprays for Palm Sunday church services. Many other Seminole women on the outlying reservations did the same. It was a clever way to make a little extra money. Betty's clients were local Episcopal, Greek Orthodox, and Lutheran churches. The fronds were very important in the annual religious services. Some of the denominations even blessed the fronds before carrying them in procession into their sanctuaries. Sometimes extra palm leaves were burned, and the ashes were saved to be used for Ash Wednesday the following year. The churches also ordered small pin-up crosses to give to hospital patients to wear or pin on their walls on Palm Sunday. "Sure it's a lot of hard work," Betty told a reporter, "but I enjoy it. It gives me a chance to get away from the city in the forest where I can loaf a little . . . and it is for the churches" (Davis n.d.).

She packed her machete on her job as coordinator of the Seminole community health services, which took her to the rural Big Cypress and Brighton Reservations. On the long drive, when she saw a good stand of palmettos, she would pull over, park, and head off into the bushes. She related the dangers that could befall the unwary harvester: "You've got to know where to step because rattlers make their homes on the ground under the palmettos, but they usually rattle before you get too close" (Davis n.d.). The palm fronds and sweet-smelling palm bloom were bundled and tied into "lots," each of which was priced at thirty dollars.

In the next tribal election in 1974, Howard Tommie, the Bird clan incumbent, was ousted by James E. Billie, the dynamic, thirty-five-year-old Vietnam veteran who was a member of Tommie's Bird clan. This was the same James Billie that Betty had protected in the late 1940s when his life had been threatened by the elders because he was half-white. This was also the same James Billie who had "lost" his school shoes in the rock pit!

Betty continued with her clinic assignment but also, at Chairman Billie's request, spent some time talking at schools during the day and accepted speaking invitations to attend club meetings at night. As a result, Betty became well known in the community for being a Seminole spokeswoman, a former chief, and a talented storyteller. She was the one Seminole individual that people could say that they had met. She has a fine rapport with audiences. She doesn't hold anything back—she tells it like it was and is. People feel that they know Betty Mae Jumper.

In 1983, at James Billie's suggestion, Betty stepped in to aid the floundering *Alligator Times* newspaper, soon renamed the *Seminole Tribune*. In January 1984, she became its editor-in-chief and soon the director of the newly created Seminole Communications Department. She began her tenure at the biweekly publication with a staff of two; one employee answered the phone and typed, and another took photographs.

Today, the *Seminole Tribune* is one of the best newspapers in Indian country, winning awards from the Native American Journalism Association every year. There is a staff of eight which includes three reporters. There are also nineteen contributing writers. Betty has been involved with the newspaper for two decades.

Betty buried Moses, Sr., her long-suffering, alcoholic husband, on January 2, 1993. In recent years, she has had more than her share of health problems. In 1995, faced with a future in a wheelchair if she didn't have operations to correct her legs with knee replacements, she checked herself into a hospital in Virginia and had both legs operated on during the same visit! In 1997 she had a mastectomy. In 1998 she fractured her arm in a freak accident at the tribal headquarters. In late 1999 she was diagnosed with colon cancer and began daily chemotherapy treatments. Nonetheless, she has kept her positive attitude and continues to be involved with the *Seminole Tribune*.

Betty's office is located on the second floor of the Seminole Tribe's new headquarters. And Betty herself keeps up with times: she has her own Web site (www.seminoletribe.com) because, as Peter Gallagher, manager of the tribe's Internet, stated, "we were getting plummeted with e-mails, people all over the world asking questions about Betty Mae. The sheer volume made it sensible to create her own Internet page" (McDonald 1998).

She is a devout Christian. Sometimes she uses her position to editoralize, to council, to inform, to preach: "If you don't have God in your life, you can't lead your life. . . . Think before it's too late. If you need help with a problem, go to the Christian people. In Hollywood, at the Chickee Church, we have lots of Christians who are willing to come to you if you call."

Betty has been rewarded for her pioneering efforts among her own people and for enriching Florida culture with her vivid descriptions of Seminole folktales. She received the Florida Folk Heritage Award in 1994, but her proudest moment came when she received an honorary doctorate of humane letters from Florida State University that same year. Honored by many women's organizations, she says to all women pursuing a career: "Do not let hardships stand in your way. Set small goals and work toward them, even if it's only fifteen minutes a day."

With all that Betty Mae Jumper has accomplished in her life, it is no exaggeration to say that she is a legend in her own time.

Epilogue

Looking down from her modern office, over land she walked bare-foot as a child at her grandmother's side, Betty Mae Jumper daydreams . . .

At times my memory goes back to the days when I used to see old people sit around a campfire. After the evening meal is over, children gather around for older people to tell them stories. This was the way that young people were taught the rules of life and their clan's ways. I am glad to say that this helped me to live and learn and to abide by the outside world's rules and laws as well.

Before we learned how to work within the system, people liked to see us wrestle alligators, make patchwork, operate a few stores, and work in commercial tourist villages where people pay to go see Indians. As long as we were there, people liked to see us. But we learned how to fight for our rights the same as anyone else.

Some people still like to see us as we were back in the 1920s or 1930s. But many young people are interested in a higher standard of living, as in the outside world. The money we make from cigarettes and bingo goes into tribal improvements so in the future our younger generation doesn't have to sit by roads trying to sell little baskets or dolls.

Today there are 2,900 Seminoles on six reservations. They live in prosperous times. In addition to the lucrative tax-free smoke shops and gaming, the tribe is involved with such business activities as vegetable and citrus growing and the production of its own Micco airplane. Every tribal member (man, woman, and child) receives a monthly dividend check for $2,000 from these tribal enterprises. Other monies go toward tribal education, medical needs, and reservation projects and construction.

The tribe's prosperity is apparent as one looks down from the rooftop of the tribal headquarters building, four stories of blue-green glass. The grounds are lushly landscaped with native vegetation; there is a reflecting pool out front, and a helicopter pad sits on the roof. A new housing subdivision abuts this building, while down the street is the modern clinic that bears Betty Mae Jumper's name. A multistory education building and senior citizen facility addresses the Hollywood community's needs in the new millennium. Similar facilities, including a banking center, have been built on the other, more isolated reservations. The tribe is in good hands and confident about the future.

Like the tribe, Betty herself has has come a long way from adversity. Despite many obstacles, she obtained an education and had a successful nursing career. More recently, she wrote three books.

And with the Wagon—Came God's Word (1985) is a poignant discussion of the coming of Christianity to the Seminole Tribe. The first book written by a Florida Seminole, it is the saga of Oklahoma Creeks who arrived in Florida bearing tales of a new God, which eventually led a traditional bundle carrier into a pond, from which he emerged a Christian. Betty's own grandfather, who pioneered Christianity in the tribe, gave her the topic for her first publication.

Legends of the Seminoles (1994) contains vivid tales of clan, custom, and cunning animals that were passed down to Betty by her grandmother, Mary Tustenuggee Tiger. They were exquisitely illustrated with the paintings of Florida artist Guy LaBree. Betty explained in the introduction: "These stories are very old, but have never been written down. If the oldest people on the reservation were to die, without leaving them for others to learn, then our culture would be gone, too" (Jumper 1994:12).

With the publication of *A Seminole Legend: The Life of Betty Mae Tiger Jumper*, Betty has three books in print. She worked on the handwritten manuscript from around 1953, when the Florida Seminoles began pulling together to combat their termination proceedings by the government, through the early 1970s. The lined sheets of spiral notebook paper were buried, typed up, buried again, and were moved from office to office.

In the mid-1970s, a fire ravaged Betty's house, destroying all the mementos and keepsakes that she held dear and had kept carefully packed in a metal oil barrel (to protect them from bugs and hurricanes). The fire started in the Jumpers' old television set, which Moses, Sr., had left on while the family was out, and quickly engulfed their old wooden house. The Jumpers came home to smoking ruins. Much of the material destroyed in the fire would have been invaluable to this publication: telegrams of congratulations, newspaper clippings, photographs, Betty's diploma from Cherokee, her nursing training certificate, notice of her appointment to the National Council on Indian Opportunity (signed by Richard M. Nixon), bundles of letters from Mrs. Stranahan and Mrs. Abbey, her doll from school that she had kept on her bed.

Betty has not had an easy life. She has fought for many things. Her first battle was to obtain an education for herself; later, she championed the education of the Seminole people. Betty's Indian name—given to her by her grandmother, Mary Tiger, when she was very small—is Pa-Ta-Kee. It means "Soldier." Betty has lived up to her name time and time again, fighting against ignorance and prejudice, fighting to preserve the oral heritage, fighting to save the Florida Indians from disease and death, and to lead them to a life with Christ, her literal Savior.

Bibilography

American Eagle. 1935. "Big Cypress Indians Aroused Hold Pow-Wow and Refuse to Recognize Peace Conference at West Palm Beach between Government Agents and Indians of Small Group." April 11. Estero, Fla.: Koreshan Unity.

Asheville Carolina Times. 1940. "4 Seminole Indians Official Visitors at Cherokee Fair." October 8.

Beebe, George. 1946. "White Man's Ways Lure Seminoles." *Miami Herald*, January 14.

Bellamy, Jeanne. 1954. "Seminole Points Out People's Dissensions." *Miami Herald*, December 13.

Belvin, B. Frank. n.d. [1955]. *The Tribes Go Up*. Atlanta: Southern Baptist Convention, Home Mission Board.

Brown, Dan. n.d. "But They Didn't Complain. Indians Had Cold Nights as Winds Swept Chickees." *Miami Herald*. Ft. Lauderdale: Sheldon Pressbook, Broward County Historical Commission.

Buswell, James Oliver III. 1972. "Florida Seminole Religious Ritual: Resistance and Change." Ph.D. diss., St. Louis University. Ann Arbor, Mich.: University Microfilms.

Casey, John C., and William Bowlegs. 1853. *Census of 1850–1853*. Tulsa: John C. Casey Papers, Gilcrease Museum.

Clark, Betty Savage. 1999a. Conversation with Patsy West. Telephone. February 15.

———. 1999b. Correspondence with Patsy West, February 19.

———. 1999c. Correspondence with Patsy West, March 7.

Collier County News. 1936. "Seminoles End Green Corn Dance and Head for Home." June 11.

Committee of Seminole Indians. 1953. "Report of Meeting Held with Area Office Officials Relative to Resolution 108, and an Expression of the Wishes of the Seminole Indians Relative to Proposed Legislation." October 16. Dania, Fla.: Seminole Agency.

Creel, Lorenzo D. 1911. "Report of Special Agent of the Seminole Indians in Florida to the Commissioner of Indian Affairs." Parts 1 and 2. Typescript. [Received by the Office of Indian Affairs, June 27, 1911.] Washington, D.C.

Daly, Jim. 1956a. "Indian Wives Adopt White Woman's Ways." *Ft. Lauderdale Daily News*, August 1. Ft. Lauderdale: Sheldon Pressbook, Broward County Historical Commission.

———.1956b. "Indians Strive to Learn Ways of Modern Life. Seminoles Accept Reality." *Ft. Lauderdale Daily News*, June 17. Ft. Lauderdale: Sheldon Pressbook, Broward County Historical Commisssion.

———. n.d. "Indians Given Delux Teepees." *Ft. Lauderdale Daily News.* Ft. Lauderdale: Sheldon Pressbook, Broward County Historical Commission.

Davis, Jim. n.d. [1970s]. "Palm Gathering Once-a-Year Job for Seminole." *Ft. Lauderdale Daily News.*

deVane, Albert. 1955. Letter to D. B. McKay, October 5. Avon Park, Fla.: Albert deVane Papers, Highlands County.

———. 1978. *DeVane's Early Florida History.* Vol. 1, 340–42. Sebring: Sebring Historical Society.

Edwards, John H. [asst. secy.]. 1926. Letter to the attorney general, April 15. Stranahan Papers, Jane Kirkpatrick Collection, Ft. Lauderdale Historical Society.

Flagg, Harold. 1954. "Osceola's Lifestory Told in Seminole Indian Production." *Ft. Lauderdale Daily News*, January 23.

Florida Federation of Women's Clubs. [ca. 1948] "The Seminoles Today." Typescript. W. Stanley Hanson Papers, Seminole/Miccosukee Photographic Archive, Ft. Lauderdale.

Ft. Lauderdale Daily News. 1935. "Seminole Girls Write of School and Camp Work." October 11.

———. 1936a. "Battleground of Seminoles to Become Theater Tonight When Scions of Once Warlike Tribe Take Actors Parts." March 14.

———. 1936b. "Really Hot." July 21.

———. 1936c. "Seminole Children Enjoy Easter Outing." April 14.

———. 1936d. "Seminole Children Observe Mothers Day during Week." May 9.

———. 1936e. "Seminole Girls Write of School and Camp Work." October 11.

———. 1936f. "Seminoles Write Exercises about Their Daily Life for Night School Classes." May 8.

———. 1937a. "First Children's Story Hour Attracts Large Throng; Group of Seminoles Aid in Program." January 18.

———. 1937b. "Three Youthful Seminoles to Attend Carolina School." January 22.

———. 1937c. "Indian Girls Are Complimented by School Teachers." May 12.

———. 1945. "Young Seminole Indian Brave on Iwo Jima Finds Dream of Shooting Japs Comes True." March 29.

———. 1949. "Friends Start Indian Welfare Plan." October 29.

———. 1955a. "Governor's Aid Sought in Fund Drive. Housing Is Major Aim of Indian Aid Group." November 25. Ft. Lauderdale: Sheldon Pressbook. Broward County Historical Commission.

———. n.d. [1955b]. "Seminole Aid Group Plans Housing Drive." [No month, no day]. Ft. Lauderdale: Sheldon Pressbook, Broward County Historical Commission.

———. 1956a. "In 40 Easy Payments." November 3. Ft. Lauderdale: Sheldon Pressbook, Broward County Historical Commission.

———. 1956b. "Meeting Monday to Push Home Program for Indians." January 27. Ft. Lauderdale: Sheldon Pressbook, Broward County Historical Commission.

———. 1956c. "She Taught Seminoles How to Live Modern." Ft. Lauderdale: Sheldon Pressbook, Broward County Historical Commission.

———. n.d.a. [1956]. "Seminoles to Ride 'Em. Indian Rodeo Gate to Aid United Fund." Ft. Lauderdale: Sheldon Pressbook, Broward County Historical Commission.

———. n.d.b. [1956]. "Indian Rodeo Cash $1,378." Ft. Lauderdale: Sheldon Pressbook, Broward County Historical Commission.

———. 1958. "Temperature Plunge Finds Seminoles Unprotected." February 14. Ft. Lauderdale: Sheldon Pressbook, Broward County Historical Commission.

———. 1959a. "Seminole Estates Opens." [November 11]. Ft. Lauderdale: Sheldon Pressbook, Broward County Historical Commission.

———. n.d.b. [1959]. "Seminoles Praised for Achievements." [ca. November 11].

———. 1960a. "You Too, Can Help the Indians." December 18.

———. 1960b. "Reservation Casino Spurned by Seminoles." December 18.

———. 1970. "Betty Mae Jumper on Indian Unit to Help Coordinate Federal Programs." September 1.

Ft. Myers Press. 1907a. "Indian Chief Threatening! 'Kill White Man Ojus.'" March 7.

———. 1907b. "Grave Robber Indicted." March 28.

Friends of the Seminoles. n.d. [ca. 1955]. "For Only $1.00 You Can Be a Friend of the Seminoles." Flier. Stranahan Papers, Friends of the Seminoles, Ft. Lauderdale Historical Society.

Gallagher, Peter B. 1994. "Introduction." *Legends of the Seminoles*, by Betty Mae Jumper. Sarasota: Pineapple Press.

Glass, Ian. 1967. "Squaw Now 'Big Chief' of Seminole Braves." *Miami News*, May 9.

Griffith, Carolanne. 1970. "Chief Betty Mae Jumper Likes 'Lib' for All." *Ft. Lauderdale Daily News*, December 18.

Hanson, W. Stanley. 1943. Letter to Ethel Cutler Freeman, May 23. Ethel Cutler Freeman Papers. National Anthropological Archives, Smithsonian Institution.

Hogan, Frank. n.d.a. [1956]. "5 Children Helpless Pawns in Clash of Two Cultures." *Ft. Lauderdale Daily News.* Ft. Lauderdale: Sheldon Pressbook, Broward County Historical Commission.

———. n.d.b. [1956]. "Nation to Get Seminole Story." *Ft. Lauderdale Daily News.* Ft. Lauderdale: Sheldon Pressbook, Broward County Historical Commission.

House of Representatives, U.S. 1953. House Congressional Resolution 108. 83rd Cong., 1st sess., August 3. Washington, D.C.: Government Printing Office.

Jones, Duane. n.d. [1957]. "Graduate Moses Gets Scholarship." *Miami Herald.* Ft. Lauderdale: Sheldon Pressbook, Broward County Historical Commission.

Jumper, Betty Mae. 1939. Letter to Mrs. [Ivy] Stranahan, February 1. Stranahan Papers, Ft. Lauderdale Historical Society.

———. 1941. Letter to Mrs. [Ivy] Stranahan, April 4. Stranahan Papers, Ft. Lauderdale Historical Society.

———. 1945a. Letter to Mrs. [Erma] Abbey, February 7. Stranahan Papers, Friends of the Seminoles, Ft. Lauderdale Historical Society.

———. 1945b. Letter to Mrs. [Erma] Abbey, December 16. Stranahan Papers, Friends of the Seminoles, Ft. Lauderdale Historical Society.

———. n.d.a. [ca. 1946]. Interview with Ivy C. Stranahan. Stranahan Papers, Friends of the Seminoles, Ft. Lauderdale Historical Society.

———. n.d.b. [after 1946]. Letter to Mrs. [Ivy] Stranahan. Stranahan Papers, Friends of the Seminoles, Ft. Lauderdale Historical Society.

———. 1947. Handwritten transcript of a speech, April. Stranahan Papers, Friends of the Seminoles, Ft. Lauderdale Historical Society.

———. 1985. *And with the Wagon—Came God's Word.* Hollywood, Fla.: Seminole Communications Department, Seminole Tribe of Florida.

———. 1994. *Legends of the Seminoles.* Sarasota: Pineapple Press.

———. 1995. "Brighton's Heritage." In "Reflections" column, by Patsy West, no. 95, seventh in a series. September 1. *Seminole Tribune.*

———. 1997. "First Days in Dania." *Seminole Tribune,* May 23.

———. 1998a. "Christmas Doll." *Seminole Tribune,* December 18.

———. 1998b. "God Answers Prayers and Church Survives." *Seminole Tribune,* October 30.

———. 1998c. "Seminole Warrior," *Seminole Tribune,* April 17.

———. 1999. "Hurricane Bird." *Seminole Tribune,* October 22.

———. 2001. Manuscript.

Jumper, Betty Mae, and Alice Osceola, eds. 1961a. *Seminole Indian News,* August 10.

———. 1961b. *Seminole Indian News,* September 6.

———. 1961c. *Seminole Indian News,* October.

Kelly, Bella. 1970. "Woman Indian Chief Works for Progress." In "Focus" column. *Miami News,* October 13.

Kersey, Harry A., Jr. 1974. "The Seminole Uprising." *Florida Anthropologist* 27: 49–58.

———. 1975a. "The Case of Tom Tiger's Horse: An Early Foray into Indian Rights." *Florida Historical Quarterly* 53: 306–18.

———. 1975b. *Pelts, Plumes and Hides: White Traders among the Seminole Indians, 1870–1930.* Gainesville: University of Florida Press.

———. 1996. *An Assumption of Sovereignty: Social and Political Transformation among the Florida Seminoles, 1953–1979.* Lincoln: University of Nebraska Press.

Kirk, Cooper, and Patricia Cunningham. 1981. *Broward Legacy* 4, nos. 1 and 2 (Winter/Spring): 30–40.

Lamme, Vernon. 1948. Letter to *Life Magazine* [with attachments], May 30. Washington, D.C.: National Archives, Records of the Indian Arts and Crafts Board.

Liss, Robert. 1975. "Backyard Talk, Cookouts Lured Seminole Voters." *Miami Herald,* May 12.

MacCauley, Clay. 1887. "The Seminole Indians in Florida." In *Fifth Annual Report of the Bureau of Ethnology*, 469–513. Washington, D.C.: Government Printing Office.

McDonald, Dan, 1998a. "Lost in Fire, Awards Re-issued to Family: Howard Tiger's War Metals." *Seminole Tribune*, April 17.

———. 1998b. "New Seminole Site: www.bettymae.com." *Seminole Tribune*, September 11.

McGown, William E. 1998. *Southeast Florida Pioneers: The Palm and Treasure Coasts*. Sarasota: Pineapple Press.

Mahon, John K. 1967. *History of the Second Seminole War, 1835–1842*. Gainesville: University of Florida Press.

Marmon, Kenneth A. 1949. Letter to Mrs. Betty Mae Jumper, December 8. Stranahan Papers, Ft. Lauderdale Historical Society.

Miami Daily News. 1933. "College Girl Describes Work among Children of Seminoles." August 30.

Miami Herald. 1915. "Death Sentence Is Passed on John Ashley." April 10.

———. 1935. "End of 100 Year War of Seminoles Nearing." March 20.

———. 1936. "Seminole Indians Dedicate Baptist Church Near Dania." June 8.

———. 1945. "Indian-Missionaries Work with Seminoles." May 28.

———. n.d.a. [1950s]. "Seminole Aid Pleas Going Out. Funds Sought to Boost Building." Ft. Lauderdale: Sheldon Pressbook, Broward County Historical Commission.

———. n.d.b. [1950s]. "Seminole Family to Move into $850 House This Week." Ft. Lauderdale: Sheldon Pressbook, Broward County Historical Commission.

———. 1957. "Little Moses Jumper Having Last Laugh on School Laws." Ft. Lauderdale: Sheldon Pressbook, Broward County Historical Commission.

Miami Sun. 1937. "Seminoles to Feature in Church Service." January 1.

Milne, Richard. 1956. "Billie Charges Pretext." *Ft. Lauderdale Daily News*, [no month, no day]. Ft. Lauderdale: Sheldon Pressbook, Broward County Historical Commission.

Moore-Willson, Minnie. 1910. *The Seminoles of Florida*. Philadelphia: America Printing House.

National Anthropological Archives, Smithsonian Institution. 1906. Washington, D.C. Photo neg. no. 44,352–E.

New York Times. 1893. "The President's Holiday." April 22.

———. 1968. "Republican Presidential Candidate R. M. Nixon Deplores Plight of Indians." September 28.

———. 1970a. "Labor Department Allocates $8.4 Million in Emergency Employment Aid Funds for Public Service Jobs for Indians." September 28.

———. 1970b. "$300,000 Funded for National Congress of American Indians." November 6.

Ober, Frederick A. "Ten Days with the Seminoles." 1875. *Appleton's Journal of Literature, Science, and Art* 14 (July–December): 142–73.

Orlando Sentinel. 1969. "What the Indians Want." November 20.

Osceola, Alice. 1961. Editorial: "Save Your Breath." October.

Paulson, Beverly. n.d. "Real 'Florida Cracker' Guides Seminoles into Modern Living." *Miami Herald.* Ft. Lauderdale: Sheldon Pressbook, Broward County Historical Commission.

Pensacola Journal. 1936. "Seminole Lassies Resume Their Trip as Escort Sobers." July 20.

Revelle, Orville. n.d. "Pass in Review." *Ft. Lauderdale Daily News.*

St. Lucie County Tribune. 1907a. "Indian Chief Threatening!" March 7.

———. 1907b. March 8.

———. 1907c. March 15.

———. 1907d. April 12.

———. 1907e. April 19.

St. Petersburg Times. 1935. "Woman's Club Hears Indian Commissioner." November 30.

Seminole Agency, Florida. 1977. *Florida Seminoles Reconstructed Census Roll of 1914.* Ft. Lauderdale: William and Edith Boehmer Papers, Seminole/Miccosukee Photographic Archive.

Seminole Tribe of Florida. 1962. "Progress Report of the Seminole Tribe of Florida." April 1. Hollywood, Fla.

Senate, U.S. Senate Executive Document 139. 1888. Attachment: letter from A. W. Wilson to J. D. Atkins, November 3, 1887. 50th Cong., 1st sess.

Sheldon Pressbook [compiled by Ann Palmer (Mrs. Francis A.) Sheldon, chairwoman of the Florida Federation of Women's Clubs' Indian Division]. [1950s]. Ft. Lauderdale: Broward County Historical Commission,

———. n.d.a. [1956]. "Lady, Don't Throw Out That Furniture." Ft. Lauderdale: Broward County Historical Commission.

———. n.d.b. [1956]. "Seminole Rodeo Slated to Open 3-Day Stand." Ft. Lauderdale: Broward County Historical Commission.

———. n.d.c. [1956]. "A Twist on the Cowboys and Indians Theme. Wild Rodeo Staged by the Seminoles." Ft. Lauderdale: Broward County Historical Commission.

Smiley, Nixon. 1964. "Jim Jumper Massacre." *Miami Herald,* November 22.

Southern Baptist Convention. 1920. Home Mission Board Minutes. "Report to Dr. B. D. Grey of Special Committee to Visit Seminole Indians in Florida." January 20.

———. n.d. *Indian Resource Book.* Atlanta: Home Mission Board.

Spencer, Lucien A. 1926. Letter to commissioner of Indian Affairs [Charles H. Burke], April 9. Stranahan Papers, Jane Kirkpatrick Collection, Ft. Lauderdale Historical Society.

Starts, Captain Al. 1986. Interview with Patsy West, July 9.

Stranahan, Ivy C. [Mrs. Frank]. 1925. Letter to L. A. Spencer, October 15. Jane Kirkpatrick Collection, Ft. Lauderdale Historical Society.

Stranahan Papers. 1924. Jane Kirkpatrick Collection, Ft. Lauderdale Historical Society.

Stout, Wesley. 1965. "Jim Jumper Massacre." *Orlando Sentinel,* March 1.

Stuart News. 1956. "Indiantown Road Dedication Recalls 60 Years History." May 10.

Sturtevant, William C. 1971. "Creek into Seminole." In *North American Indians in Historical Perspective,* ed. Eleanore Burke Leacock and Nancy Oestreich Lurie, 92–128. New York: Random House.

Tampa Daily Times. 1912. "Indians Ask Reward Be Offered for Murderer." January 16.

Tiger, Howard. 1961. Letter to the editors of *Seminole Indian News* in "Tiger Roars Past Cypress" by Betty Jumper. November.

United Press International. 1961. "Seminole Scoop." October. Ft. Lauderdale: Sheldon Pressbook, Broward County Historical Commission.

U.S. Congress. 1954. *Termination of Federal Supervision over Certain Tribes of Indians, Joint Hearing before the Subcommittee of the Committees on Interior and Insular Affairs, 83rd Cong., 2nd sess. On S. 2747 and H.R. 7321, part 8, Seminole Indians of Florida,* March 1–2. Washington, D.C.: Government Printing Office.

U.S. Department of the Interior, Office of Indian Affairs. 1927. *Annual Report,* Dania, Fla.: Seminole Agency.

———. 1932. *Annual Report.* Dania, Fla.: Seminole Agency.

———. 1933. *Annual Report.* Dania, Fla.: Seminole Agency.

———. 1946. *Annual Report.* Dania, Fla.: Seminole Agency.

———. 1953. *Annual Report.* Dania, Fla.: Seminole Agency.

U.S. Indian Service. 1944. *Indians at Work* 12, no. 2 (July–August): 1.

Vinciguerra, Tom. n.d. [1956]. "Seminoles' Rodeo Offers Many Thrills." *Miami Herald.* Ft. Lauderdale: Sheldon Pressbook, Broward County Historical Commission.

West, Patsy. 1989. "Seminole Indian Settlements at Pine Island, Broward County, Florida: An Overview." *Florida Anthropologist* 32, no. 1: 43–56.

———. 1992. "The Seminole Old Tiger Tail and the Period of Isolation." *Florida Anthropologist* 45, no. 4 (December): 363–68.

———. 1995a. "Brighton's Heritage." In "Reflections" column, no. 95, 7th in a series, September 1. *Seminole Tribune.*

———. 1995b. "Brighton's Heritage: The Bitter Truth." In "Reflections" column, no. 97, 9th in a series, September 29. *Seminole Tribune.*

———. 1995c. "A Chronology of Seminole Cattle Raising Tribune since 1740." In *The Proceedings of the Florida Cattlemen's Association and the Florida Cracker Cattle Breeder's Association*, ed. Brenda J. Elliott and Joe Knetsch, March, 24–42. Kissimmee, Fla.

———. 1996. "Seminoles Honor the Daughters of the American Revolution." *Seminole Tribune*, December 20.

———. 1998a. "The Education of Tony Tommie." In "Reflections" column, no. 153, August 21. *Seminole Tribune.*

———. 1998b. *The Enduring Seminoles: From Alligator Wrestling to Ecotourism.* Gainesville: University Press of Florida.

———. 1999. "Days Of Corn Dance. Gone." Unpublished manuscript. Ft. Lauderdale.

Will, Lawrence. 1964. *Cracker History of Okeechobee.* St. Petersburg, Fla.: Great Outdoors.

Williams, Ada Coates. 1996. *Florida's Ashley Gang.* Port Salerno: Florida Classics Library.

Wilson, Beverly. 1967. "New Image for Indians." *Miami Herald*, July 30.

Index

Page numbers in italics indicate photographs.

58; public school opened to Seminoles (1947), 117, 136; and reservation youth, 164; on the reservation
(Dania), 45, 64–70; and summer
teaching volunteers, 67–68; and truant officer, 157; and USET, 163. *See
also* Cherokee Indian Boarding
School
Egmont Key, 3
Emmons, Glenn, Indian commissioner,
149
Everglades, 2, 46
Executive Order of 1911, 46

Fee and Stewart Company, 24
Fewell, Billy (Wind), 13
Fewell, Eula, 39, 69
Fewell, Juanita, 69
Fewell family, 48
First Seminole War. *See* Seminole Wars
Fisheating Creek camp, 9–11
Florida (*In-Con-Uck'seh*), 26
Florida Federation of Women's Clubs
(also FFWC Indian Welfare Com-
mittee), 47, 129
Florida Power and Light, 148
Florida State College for Women, 66
Florida State University, 170
Florida Turnpike, *94*; cut through Dania
Reservation, 143
Flournoy, John T., 22–25
folkways, Florida Seminole, 10; animal
husbandry, 43; and animals, 16; bad
medicine, 31, 40, 78; campfire, 52–
53; childbirth, children, 52–53, 55–
56; death, burial, and mourning, 13–
16, 22, 36, 126; decision making,
142; discipline, 13, 53–54; folktales/
legends, 8, 54, 68, 172–73; games,
58–63, 67; gardening, 68; ghosts, 63;
incest, 18, 55, 125; infanticide, 12,
39–44, 125–26; inheritance, 12;
looking at a stranger, 108; marriage
and divorce, 55–56; matrilineal, 48;

matrilocal residence, 18; medicine,
55; menses, 55; miscegenation, 12–
13, 15, 39–41, 72; number (sacred),
74–75; play, 73; polygyny, 18; punishment, 12, 16, 108; sickness, 14,
16; slavery, 1, 12–16; time of day, 38;
turkey, 53; uncles, role of, 53, 55–56,
59, 138; weather, 55, 74–76; whites,
55; widowhood, 36. *See also* camps;
canoes; chickees; clans; dogs; Green
Corn Dance; half-breeds; *Ho-la wa-
gus*; horses; hunting; hurricanes; languages; medicine, spiritual; medicine
men; oral history
—and food, 16, 32, 46; alligator, 53;
garfish, 53; hogs, 6, 10–11, 19–20,
36; honey, 53; major meals, 52; meat,
49–50; and nontraditional diet, 142;
preparation of, 5; sofki, 53; swamp
cabbage, 52; traditional foods missed,
111; turtles (land and water), 53
Fort Gardner, 18
Fort Lauderdale Women's Club. *See*
welfare
Fort Lauderdale Daily News, 68–69
Fort Myers News Press, 23, 69
Fort Pierce, 16, 19, 23–25
Friends of the Florida Seminoles. *See*
welfare
Friends of the Seminoles. *See* welfare
Frog clan. *See* Big Towns clan

Gallagher, Peter, 170
Gilchrist, Gov. Albert W., 35
Girtman Brothers Trading Post, 35
Glenn, Rev. James L. (special commis-
sioner), 66, 74, 128
Goat, Rev. Alfred (Oklahoma Creek),
38
Goat, Rev. Martin (Oklahoma Creek),
38, 77
Godcharles, Jeanette, 69
Gopher, Jimmie (great-uncle, "uncle,"
"grandfather") (Snake), 17, 34–44,

miscegenation. *See* folkways
missionaries and families (Oklahoma
Creek and Seminole Indians), 37–38,
81, 172; investigative committee visits
Florida (1920), 37; Brown, Jackie, 77;
Coon, Billy, 77; Goat, Rev. Alfred,
38; Goat, Rev. Martin, 38, 77; Goat,
Reverend, 27, 34; Harjo, Chitee, 77;
Harjo, Eula, 77; Harjo, Mrs. George,
77; King, Lena, *84*; King, Willie, *84*;
Marks, Amos, 76; Smith, Rev. Stan-
ley, 135; Tmomokee, Solomon, 77;
Walker, Dave, 77; Wise, Mr. and
Mrs. Arthur, 77. *See also* Indiantown
—visits to Florida by: 1907, 26–33;
1914, 36; 1916, 36; 1918, 36
Mississippi Band of Choctaw Indians,
162
Moore-Willson, Minnie (author), 21–
22, 24
Morgan, Jesse, 74
Motlow family, 48
murder, 13–16, 34–35, 74
Muscogee speakers: as formal language
users, 9, 18; influx of (1814), 8; and
Oklahoma missionaries, 26–33, 38;
people who did not speak Creek, 30;
scorned by Mikasuki speakers, 44

Nancy, Nagey, 13
narratives. *See* oral history
National Council on Indian Opportu-
nity (1970), 164–66
Native American Journalism Awards,
169
New Deal, 72–73
New River, 34, 40, 46
New York Times, 165
Nigger Jim (Little Black Snake). *See*
Jumper, Jim
Nigger Jim Scrub, 16
Ninety Mile Prairie, 11
Nixon, Richard M.: and National Con-
gress on Indian Affairs (NCIA, 1970),

165–66; and National Council on Indian Opportunity (1968), 164–66
nonreservation Indians: opposition of, to
New Deal, 73; and political differences with reservation dwellers, 138,
142; receive medical aid (1945), 122;
at termination meetings, 139. *See also*
Miccosukees; Traditional Seminoles
Northway, S. E., 147

Ober, Frederick, 9–10
Okalee Museum, 62
Okeechobee, 7, 11, 16, 27
Okeechobee Improvement Company, 18
Oklahoma, 2, 137; fear of being re-
moved to, 8, 48, 125; Florida Semi-
noles' visits to, 35; Indian Baptist
Church (Sasakwa), 77, 101; Indian
Health Service area office (Oklahoma
City), 162–63; Kiowa Teaching Hos-
pital (Lawton), 119; and missionaries
(Holdenville), 26–27; Muscogee and
Seminole Area Office, 138–39; and
nurses' field training (Shawnee), 121;
visitors from, 76–77; Wetumka, 76
oral history, 2–8; massacre at Bluefields,
13–16; about Oklahoma missionaries,
26–32; war, 3–7
Osceola, Alice Daye (Bird), *96*, 150–53
Osceola, Rev. Bill (Bird), 129, 148, 155,
158
Osceola, Rev. Billy (Bird), *91*, 154, 159;
chairman of tribal council (1957),
156
Osceola, Charlotte (née Mary) Tommie
(Snake). *See* Tommie, Mary (Charlotte)
Osceola, Laura Mae Jumper (Panther),
91, 142
Osceola, Jack (Otter), 48, 69–70, *85*
Osceola, Joe Dan (Jaudon) (Panther),
99; president of the Seminole Tribe
of Florida, Inc., 162, 164
Osceola, Martha, *93*, 148

Betty Mae Tiger Jumper is the only woman to chair the Seminole Tribe of Florida (1967–71) and is the director of Seminole Communications. She is an author, newspaper editor, storyteller, and activist, and she is the recipient of the state's Woman of the Year award, and of Florida State University's Doctor of Humane Letters.

Patsy West is an ethnohistorian who has directed a private Seminole/Miccosukee photo archive since 1972. She has written a history column for the *Seminole Tribune* since 1985, is a historic preservationist, and, with Seminole chairman James E. Billie, is coexecutive producer of "Unconquered!," a Seminole tribal documentary film series scheduled for future release. She is the author of *The Enduring Seminoles: From Alligator Wrestling to Ecotourism* (University Press of Florida, 1998), which has won two awards: in 1999, the Harry T. and Harriette V. Moore award for the best book on Florida's ethnic and cultural history, from the Florida Historical Society, and in 2000 a certificate of commendation from the American Association for State and Local History.